JOURNEY
THROUGH LENT
with MATTHEW

DAILY MEDITATIONS

ANDREW D. ROGNESS

Augsburg
MINNEAPOLIS

JOURNEYING TROUGH LENT WITH MATTHEW
Daily Meditations

Large-quantity purchases or custom editions of this book are available at a discount from the publisher. For more information, contact the sales department at Augsburg Fortress, Publishers, 1-800-328-4648, or write to: Sales Director, Augsburg Fortress, Publishers, P.O. Box 1209, Minneapolis, MN 55440-1209.

Cover photography from PhotoDisc
Cover design by Timothy W. Larson
Book design by Jessica A. Klein

ISBN 0-8066-4266-1

The paper used in this publication meets the minimum requirements of American National Standard for Information Sciences—Permanence of Paper for Printed Library Materials, ANSI Z329.48-1984. ♾ ™

Manufactured in the U.S.A.   AF 9-4266

05   04   03   02   01   1   2   3   4   5   6   7   8   9   10

Contents ⟶

Week Four

Week Five

Week Six

Week Seven

INTRODUCTION ⟶

THIS IS A GUIDEBOOK—intended to augment the immersion of your life into Jesus Christ through the Gospel of Matthew. As with any guidebook, it cannot make the journey for you. With a variety of reflections, prayers, and questions, however, it will help you on your way and challenge you to give yourself to the experience.

When I guide people in the Boundary Waters Canoe Area Wilderness in northern Minnesota, I begin each day's journey by gathering everyone at the shore next to our loaded canoes. With a map in hand, I ask the group to point out on the map where we are, to indicate the bays and islands that correspond with the squiggly lines on the map, and to determine the direction we're going. As the day's journey progresses, we take additional moments to find our bearings.

The same process is used in this book. I raise the same kind of issues, with particular concern for our orientation at the starting point and along the way. Insofar as we understand that not ourselves, but God, is at the heart and center of our reading of Matthew and of our life, our compass readings will be true. We find ourselves and the course of our lives in reference to the landscape—the life and teachings of Jesus. You can help orient yourself with this simple ancient tool: begin each day and begin each day's reading by closing your eyes, taking three slow breaths, and with each inhalation simply say to yourself, "Lord Jesus, come in."

Each day's reading concludes with a thought or a question for reflection and a prayer. The prayer is there in case you're in a rush. Take the time with each day's reading to close your eyes and let thoughts flow back and forth between yourself and God. The same can be said for the comment or question for reflection.

Except for Ash Wednesday, each day also designates a portion of Matthew's Gospel to read. Ash Wednesday has no reading because of the importance I place on not beginning a journey before finding my bearings on the map. In this instance, Ash Wednesday is given to changing our usual orientation as we read Scripture. Instead of Scripture being the object of our study, we become the object of God's transformation through Scripture.

Although this guide can be used any time of year, it assumes a forty-seven day time frame, beginning Ash Wednesday and ending the journey on Easter Sunday. If a study group is using this book, share your reflections, your insights, and your questions in a weekly discussion.

If you follow this itinerary, you will read the full Gospel of Matthew. Different areas of thought will be pointed out to heighten your awareness as you travel. However, the journey is primarily yours to make into the mind and heart of God.

Ash Wednesday: Lost and Found

T HE ASH WEDNESDAY WORSHIP SERVICE moves from confession to an act of penitence. An acrid smell of burning palm leaves hangs in the air. Moments before, smoke billowed from a few dried palm branches saved from last year's Palm Sunday service. Mesmerized by the fire curling up the fronds toward my hand, we watch the ashes fall to join the pile accumulated from past years. Now the line of people somberly makes its way up the center aisle. I am gowned in black. With solemnity I repeat again and again, "Remember, you are dust, and to dust you shall return."

My thumb and forefinger dip into the baptismal font holding the ashes. It seems wrong. I'm used to seeing pristine water there. Maybe I should have found something different to use—a clay pot, a platter tempered for ovens, anything other than the font. Ashes are polluting where crystal clear waters should be. Words of death are spoken instead of words of life. Perhaps I should soft-pedal this moment like some mortician, and speak of passing on, of eternal rest, of falling asleep into the everlasting arms. But no. The harsh truth: "You are dust."

Like a lamb led to the slaughter, each worshiper steps to the front. Eyes meet mine with trust that this ancient ritual joins us to something deeper. "Remember . . ." And I remember. Vividly, I remember singing a baptismal hymn at my brother's funeral:

> *All who believe and are baptized*
> *Shall see the Lord's salvation.*
> *Baptized into the death of Christ,*
> *We are a new creation* (LBW , #194).

Even at age twelve I could reconcile the incongruities: with tears streaming down my face, I understood my parents' choice of this hymn.

Now, instead of baptismal oil, ashes mark a cross on each forehead. Excess ashes sprinkle onto eyebrows and noses. And I remember my brother's death. I think of realities greater than my mortal body. The words do not evade eternal truths: "To dust you shall return."

"You are dust." The church, either consciously or by rote, engages the wisdom of existentialist philosophy: pushing us to come to terms with our mortality as the path to finding meaning in our lives. Others engage death and speak with morbidity, nihilism, cynicism, and despair. The church faithfully speaks of death and is strengthened by hope.

"You are dust." More than sixteen billion years ago, we're told, cosmic dust compressed into a singular mass and burst: God splitting the seams and flinging the galaxies out on divine elastic strings. My dust was there, as was yours, and it is all returning to dust. We return to the hand that flings us out, to the one whose imagination continues to intrigue and dumbfound. We are specks of dust with unbounded egos, claiming that such infinite power and being knows each of us by name. If we are conscious of what we're doing in this claim, we would run away in terror. Yet we plod on to the font of ashes. We cling to an invitation mouthed by God through Jesus. We dare to hope.

"You are dust." I speak the words with as much gentleness as I can muster. We know these words will be spoken at our funerals, so it is hard to say them without trying to soften their harshness. Even so, the taste of the words cannot be so easily seasoned as to hide their blow to our inflated egos.

"You are nothing," the words say. They call us back to the enigmatic sayings of Jesus: "Whoever would find their life will lose it, and whoever loses their life for my sake will find it" (Matt. 10:39).

For a brief moment, we are each brought to our knees—not in penitential sadness so much as humility. All the worshipers return to their seats, glancing at one another as though looking in a mirror. We are each one made by God. Each one is given life and worth by God. Each one is on a journey home to God. Without God, each one is nothing. While the smell of dust and ashes lingers in the air, for this brief moment we are fully awake to reality. God is the center of our life and of all things.

It won't be long before the ashes are brushed aside, before the service is ended, before the foreheads are washed clean. Old habits, being what they are, will lull us into the sleep that dreams of ourselves at the center of our life and our universe. But the cross remains, marking us invisibly and indelibly. Jesus knew: the death of self is the path to the resurrection and the life.

Think about the difference between studying Scripture and opening oneself to Scripture.

I give thanks, O God, for words of truth spoken in love. May the words of this reading and the words of Matthew's Gospel lead me to Jesus: the Word, the Truth, the Way, and the Life.

Week One ⟶

Thursday: Beyond Ethnic Cleansing

Read Matthew 1:1-17. *"An account of the genealogy of Jesus the Messiah, the son of David, the son of Abraham"* (v. 1).

My PARENT'S ANCESTORS all emigrated from Norway. Norwegian customs were common in our household. *Vær så god, mange tusen takk,* and *uff da,* were a part of our daily language. It was natural that from a very early age I developed ethnic pride. When my older siblings began marrying people with no trace of this heritage, I remember thinking that I, as the youngest, would be the last line of defense in preserving the purity of the strain. Yet when I fell in love, I don't remember even a fleeting thought of this prerequisite. Love is a greater force than ethnic pride, than human existence. All humans are God's children and are loved deeply by God.

Jesus was born with the finest of human pedigrees. His genealogy was established for those who considered such distinctions important. Yet John the Baptist saw through this inflated view of ethnic pride and warned those who saw their family tree as God's exclusive gift. Heritage does not define our place in God's creation. Matthew's Gospel begins with Jesus in a line of forty-two generations from Abraham and Sarah, and ends with Jesus breaking the exclusiveness of those who saw themselves as God's chosen, calling for an inclusiveness of "all nations."

I may be able to let go of an overbearing pride of Norwegian heritage; I may be able to see beyond the exclusiveness of a Jewish lineage; but I am still likely to read the Bible as though we humans are the pinnacle of God's creation and the principle motivation for God's acts. Yet I can almost imagine John the Baptist picking up a few stones in his hand, as he said, "Do not presume to say to yourselves, 'We have Abraham as our ancestor;' for I tell you, God is able from these stones to raise up children to Abraham" (Matt. 3:9). The words he spoke were in the spirit of a prophet—not his own words, but words passed on from the heart of God. Perhaps John also looked at those stones, not as a human would look at them, but as God would: primal dust of the solar system, more ancient and enduring than the infancy of the human creation. "From dust you have come and to dust you shall return" (Gen. 3:19).

Just as it is understandable that I would, in my adolescence, carry a vaunted view of being of Norwegian descent, so it is tempting for humans to maintain an adolescent view of ourselves at the center of God's universe. As our world enters the third millennium, however, God calls us to deep faith and faithful action. A population explosion that pressures the earth's environment in destructive ways, which parallels the patterns of cancerous growth, awakens us to the temptation to define God from our human perspective. As we read Matthew, we do so from the perspective of the mind and heart of God.

Along with John, we pick up a handful of stones and remember that "The earth is God's and the fullness thereof" (Ps. 24:1). Looking at the universe from the mind and heart of God, full of creative love, full of billions of years in the making, we can imagine the ruminations of a loving heart:

"What is the place of these human creatures? How shall I help them see their place in the universe? How shall I help them move from archaic notions of deity and from vaunted notions of themselves? Can they be taught in time, to let go of being at the center? How might they expand the imagination of their minds and the compassion of their hearts, and discover the true nature of their soul?"

◆◆◆◆◆

Ponder the questions in the paragraph above.

Help us to look at the world through your eyes, O God. You have made us to care for all that you have made and love. May we do so.

FRIDAY: GOD IS WITH US

Read Matthew 1:18-25. *". . . and they shall name him Emmanuel, which means 'God is with us' "* (v. 23).

WHEN I WAS TEN AND IN FOURTH GRADE, something happened to my hearing. Antibiotics didn't solve the hearing loss. All winter long my hearing was impaired to the point that I needed to sit in the front of my class in order to hear the teacher. My parents, my physician, and I were in a holding pattern, waiting to see what would happen. Because my grandmother had experienced diminished hearing at an early age, my family wondered if that would be my fate as well.

One day in early spring on my way home for lunch, I was slogging through the melting snow where water was running in the gutter. Forty years later, I can still go to the exact spot where my ears began to open, and where I heard again the wonderful sounds of water squishing and trickling under my feet. I ran the next two blocks home to tell Mom the good news: I could hear fully again. Being a mother, she needed the reassurance of proof. As lunch was served, she stood behind me whispering "Andrew." As I turned in response, my joy for hearing was matched by her joy in being heard.

The sounds of God are and always have been present. God is immanent—with us. With the birth of Jesus, it is as though our ears fully opened to the mind and heart of God. Our hearts leap for joy in the knowledge that we hear God's voice speak words of love and forgiveness and empowerment.

Joseph listened to God's word and was steadfast in his commitment to Mary. God whispered to him in a dream and Joseph's hearing gave God joy. We, too, hear the voice of God who is with us. And as we listen and obey, we, too, give God joy.

God speaks to us in the life and teachings of Jesus. It is our choice to listen. A person who teaches the skill of active listening told me that we hear everything; we may choose not to listen to everything, however. We are constantly filtering out sounds. Take a moment right now to listen to everything you can hear. Unconsciously we screen out all kinds of sounds while we focus on what's at hand.

Just as with our intent we can alter what we hear, so also can we choose to listen to God. God speaks, is heard, and is listened to as we read the Gospels. Rather than screen out God's words, we listen for how God speaks to us through the timeless words of Jesus. Your picking up this book and daily reading of Matthew indicates your interest in listening to God. Just as daily exercise increases our strength and stamina, so, too, will daily spiritual listening increase our closeness to God. Reading Scripture, devotionals, and prayer are helpful exercises. We can also use our daily routines for times of meditation; for example, solo commutes without the radio on, a daily walk, or saying a prayer every time we check the time of day.

God listens to us. God rejoices as we hear. God is always with us. It may not always feel that way. But my feelings sometimes belie reality. Though I may fall asleep to the presence of God, God stays with me and speaks to me. Though I may not listen to God, God is faithful in speaking words of love and hope. The seeds of life and love are planted even when the snows of winter make them invisible. God is always present. Love undergirds our very being. Hearts once frozen can flow again. It is not God who comes to us. It is we who awaken to God.

◆•◈•◆

What feels dead in your life and is in need of renewal? Talk with God about it. Journal your thoughts.

Love of my heart, awaken me from slumber. Come with the winter's end, and burst forth with new life again. Amen.

SATURDAY: OUT OF THE ORDINARY

Read Matthew 2:1-15. *Wise men from the East came to Jerusalem, asking, "Where is the child who has been born king of the Jews? For we observed his star at its rising, and have come to pay him homage"* (vv. 1-2).

ON A TRIP WEST, my wife and I and our two teenage sons stopped at the Great Sand Dunes National Park in southern Colorado.

I was amazed at how difficult and draining it was to climb to the first high peak on a hot summer's day. The journey of the wise men two thousand years ago across the Syrian desert was a thousand times more treacherous. In spite of the dangers, expense, and time required, they were compelled by a celestial event to set out, hoping to discover something that would justify their eccentricity to family and friends. I admire their willingness to risk so much, to play out their reading of the night sky and discover if their notions had any merit.

The wise men who came to worship Jesus are not the only ones to be drawn forward by God. In the book *The Feminine Face of God*, there are many anecdotes of women who had a significant experience of faith, mystery, and the divine in their early years. When they tried to tell others about their profound faith encounters, they were met with skepticism and unbelief. After that, many of them kept their experiences to themselves. Some were able to find acceptability only outside the confines of their religious institutions. "However, even when no reinforcement was offered, or when the child was subjected to ridicule or punishment for what she had experienced, this first direct connection with the divine was acknowledged by most of the women as the 'seedbed' for the unfolding of the sacred in their lives."

When my son was four, he and I were walking along an unofficial path above some bluffs in Governor Dodge State Park in southwest Wisconsin. He was walking in front of me, negotiating roots, rocks, and unevenness. More significantly, the path was close to the edge of twenty-foot and thirty-foot drops. At about the same time that I thought to myself, "I should be holding his hand," he tripped, falling in the direction of one of those edges. Miraculously, and to my great surprise and relief, he didn't fall. I didn't see how it was possible that he didn't fall, but he turned, looked up at me and said, "Dad, I felt like the hand of God held me and kept me from falling." I told him I could imagine that was true. I can still feel my irresponsibility and the terror of the moment. And I wonder if he recalls the sense of the hand of God that holds him.

Our lives hold infinite possibility for encounters of the divine. In spite of inhibitions and forgetfulness of the presence of the divine, mystic events break in upon our consciousness, and compel us to pay attention.

Our communities are full of sages with untold experiences of profound mystery and unusual encounters with God. Many of us have untold stories of our own. Compelling thoughts and intuitions come "out of the blue" or at times of need. Dreams may communicate an important truth. An unexpected call or letter or encounter may be more than coincidence. A sermon where God speaks through a preacher with exactly what was needed for someone's life. Clear images come to mind through prayer or meditation. The action of an animal or the "forces" of nature moves us. A clutching at the heart and the tugs of conscience lead us. Most of us have encounters with a "star" that leads us and that we believe few others can see or understand. When we follow, we discover the manger, Jesus, and home at our journey's end.

What have been important encounters with God in your life? What was your experience and your response?

Loving God, may my life journey be wide awake to your presence and my steps quick to follow the stars you place in my night sky to lead me to Jesus.

First Sunday in Lent: The Face of Humanity

Read Matthew 2:16-23. *A voice was heard in Ramah, wailing and loud lamentation, Rachel weeping for her children; she refused to be consoled, because they are no more* (v. 18).

My eyes filled with tears today for Joshua Richard— someone I do not know. His photo revealed a sunny smile and innocent eyes that drew me into reading his obituary: "Age 5. Died unexpectedly from a rare and undetected birth defect." The column went on lovingly to describe what every five-year-old should be. I felt the sorrow of his parents, and how my heart would have broken if I had experienced such a loss.

The aftermath of the wise men's visit to Herod meant the slaughter of untold numbers of infants in Bethlehem. It happened to so many and so long ago, that it is easy for us to be numbed by the scope of the atrocity and read on quickly. We almost make it, except that one voice is heard in Ramah— mother Rachel. We cannot make it past the sound of her heart breaking for her children who are no more. We want to believe that it could never happen again, but Rachel's lament rises through the pages of history and cannot be silenced.

Joseph Stalin was the most barbarous dictator of the twentieth century—responsible for the deaths of more innocents than even Hitler. He was reputed to have said that when one person dies it is a sorrow, when two or three die it is a tragedy, when a thousand die, it is a statistic. The voice of Rachel prevents us from a callous reading of biblical history. We are forced to feel one broken heart and cannot be dulled by a gross statistic.

We are bright, intelligent, and sensitive people, we of North America. We are not ignorant of the enormity and urgency of the many issues that press upon us, and we are not powerless. It is the wisdom of Scripture and our faith that knows that when an issue is given a face and a name, our hearts melt into deeds of compassion and justice. Our response to homelessness may change when we discover an old friend's mental illness has caused him or her to be one among the thousands. Judgmental positions regarding hetero-sexual cohabitation without benefit of marriage or concern-ing homosexuality can dramatically change when the "issue" becomes one's child. Pictures and personal stories coming out of Africa personify the enormity of their AIDS epidemic and the plight of millions of those orphaned. The cry of Rachel is heard again, and we cannot turn our backs. The love and will of God swells within our hearts. Through countless deeds of mercy, we who call Jesus "Lord," with our acts of compassion, dignity, and hope, become the human face through whom God's love is given.

At least one escaped the slaughter in Bethlehem. I can imagine it likely that as he grew, Jesus heard the stories of his early years. The cry of Rachel was remembered, told again and again in the hopes that something like Bethlehem, or Auschwitz, or the Gulag, or My Lai, or Littleton, would never ever happen again. I can imagine that as Jesus held chil-dren in his lap, and as he told us that inasmuch as we have done it to the least of these, we have done it to him, perhaps he was remembering the playmates he might have had in Bethlehem, remembering Rachel's cry, and willing his face onto every human.

As you read the newspaper, or as you watch televised news, try this: Say a simple prayer with each item—even a simple, "God, in your mercy, hear my prayer." Reflect on how that changes your interaction with the news.

Lord Jesus, help me always to remember that each person in this world is your child, and that each person is loved by you. May my deeds be yours and my words be those you would speak as I bring your tender love to all those who are in need of love, encouragement, and prayer.

Monday: Let it Be

Read Matthew 3:1-17. *"I need to be baptized by you, and do you come to me?" But Jesus answered him, "Let it be so now; for it is proper for us in this way to fulfill all righteousness"* (vv. 14-15).

"Form follows function follows faith." This was the kernel of wisdom given to us by the consultant our parish hired to advise us on our building needs. Begin with your faith. Structure the practice of your faith—your rituals, your programs, and your life together—according to what best serves your faith. Upon this foundation, let your physical structure, your staff, and your governance take shape. We were helped to see that property and rituals should be the servant of faith, and not the other way around. Jesus began his public ministry with faith in a loving God at the heart, at the center of his being. All else followed.

As Matthew's Gospel is read, it is helpful to keep this in mind. What guides Jesus in each encounter is based upon the foundation of faith in a loving God. John realized that Jesus did not need to be baptized and stated this clearly. Jesus' response indicates he understood what John was saying. More important to Jesus than the appropriateness of the ritual, however, is the wisdom that seeks to follow paths of right-eousness. It is as though he is saying, "My life is given to God, and the ritual of baptism is a sign of giving myself to God's ways. The ritual is secondary to the underlying truth it represents. My participating in this ritual will further the truth." Function follows faith. It is the same principle by which Jesus later challenges, overturns, renews, or initiates other rituals.

When a Christian or a Christian community follows the principle of building our thoughts and actions and forms on the foundation of faith in a loving God, we follow the path of Jesus. Even mundane issues are guided by this to keep the issues from becoming a problem. My congregation in Madison worked through such an issue in a way that left a lasting impression and taught a valuable lesson always sum-marized by the clarion call, "Remember the carpet." The sanctuary needed new carpeting. The issue of contention that developed was its color. At the time we were reaching an impasse on this decision, Parker Palmer, a Quaker and author, addressed one of our adult forums. He spoke of how Quakers viewed voting as a form of violence, and then described how they would use consensus as a process for all decisions at all levels of their church bodies. We were intrigued and decided, "Why not? Let's try this in choosing a color of the carpet."

One of the essential elements of this process is to honor the "inner light," the presence of God in each person that may at times speak through one voice in calling on everyone else to see things differently. When everyone who wanted to be a part of this process gathered, we explained how the discussion would be led and how we would move toward consensus. We let everyone know that any one person could stand opposed to the whole, assuming they felt strongly that building consensus for a color was not what God wanted. Then we proceeded.

Everyone quickly saw the humor in thinking God would care whether or not the carpet was burgundy or forest green, and people began saying things like, "You know, it's just something we're going to walk on." The process went quickly, and we learned the wisdom gained when you apply the formula, "Form follows function follows faith." Moreover, we were given the gift of light-hearted wisdom that could often say, "Remember the carpet."

Jesus followed God's path in deciding to submit to the ritual of baptism. God's response for Jesus' action was immediate: "This is my son in whom I am well pleased" (Matt. 3:17). Whenever our paths are taken because our faith leads us, the heart of God speaks once again, "Ah, my child, you please me."

———

When have you experienced a "carpet" moment, when you were caught up in unimportant things, only to be called back to the more important issues of faith?

Lord Jesus, may my love for you be at the heart and center of everything I do and say, so that as this day comes to a close, you will be able to say, "Well done, good and faithful servant."

TUESDAY: A DEVIL OF A TIME

Read Matthew 4:1-11. *Then Jesus was led up by the Spirit into the wilderness to be tempted by the devil* (v. 1).

DR. FRANK LAKE, a psychiatrist from Great Britain and author of *Clinical Theology*, led a group of twenty of us in an exercise he called "The Brandenburg Concerto." One person took the role of someone they were counseling; another, their counselor. At first these two were the only ones who spoke, role-playing a counseling session. The rest of us were assigned the roles of others who were a part of the life of the counselee. We were to listen and imagine what the thoughts and feelings of our character would be in response to the unfolding description of the counselee's situation. Dr. Lake assigned someone to empathize with the counselor, and someone to empathize with the counselee. They sat next to their "alter-egos." Then came other key players taking the roles of family members and coworkers in the situation. Because I was toward the end of the assigned list, I wondered what he would do as he ran out of roles to assign. He had a broader imagination than mine. The three before me were each assigned as a member of the Trinity. Then Dr. Lake came to me and said he wanted me to take the role of the devil. Everyone chuckled at this, but because I had once been a villain in a musical, I thought I had some practice at this sort of thing and was up to the job.

From my diabolical perspective, I listened to the unfolding story. It was easy to see how the devil would make use of this situation of struggle, conflict, and pain. When the role-playing of a counseling session ended, the rest of us shared our thoughts from the perspective assigned us. My observations were clearly evil, and I was unsettled by how easily they came, and how a part of me relished the role. It was as though I had been given permission to play out what happens to each one of us. We would like to think that temptation comes from without and not from within.

One of the best known lines of the cartoon character Pogo is his observation, "We have met the enemy and it is us." In the same vein, I was once told by someone involved in creating a communal living situation for the Benedictine Sisters in Madison, Wisconsin, that the most difficult thing in joining an intentional Christian community is that no matter what community you become a part of, the most difficult person for you to deal with is always present. When I first heard this, it took a moment for me to catch on to what was meant: the most difficult person is always yourself. The devil has no power in our lives, except as an ally for the forces of evil. Temptations have strength when I give them strength.

I would like to externalize my temptations by thinking of them coming from forces outside myself. That leaves me more in the role of an innocent victim, but it leaves me more vulnerable to the power of temptation. The fact is, a temptation that comes from without is recognizable only because something within has already had the idea. Adam and Eve would not have heard the whispering of the serpent unless they had already been wondering about the fruit of the Tree of Good and Evil. Jesus' struggle with the devil was real because the temptations were issues he would be struggling with: the power to create miracles, political power, and the power to be spectacular and preserve his own life.

Temptations do come. There is no stopping that. How Jesus handled the temptations provides us with a valuable lesson.

First, he acknowledged their reality. Once the temptation was spelled out, Jesus responded in a similar manner to each one. Jesus deferred to God, giving God center stage, releasing himself into the power of God. With each temptation, Jesus made reference to God, and all the power of the tempter's voice was silenced. Just as a sound wave can be silenced by broadcasting an exact opposite sound wave, we stand a chance in our encounters with temptations insofar as we are able to name that which tempts us, and to call on God to come to our aid.

Ask God to call to your conscious mind the places in your life where temptations are the strongest. Ask God to show you how to handle the temptations.

When temptations come, may I then remember, O God, that you stand with me. Help me be honest with you, so that I am better able to hear your voice. Strengthen me to do your will.

WEDNESDAY: WHATEVER IT TAKES

Read Matthew 4:12-25. *So his fame spread throughout all Syria, and they brought to him all the sick, those who were afflicted with various diseases and pains, demoniacs, epileptics, and paralytics, and he cured them. And great crowds followed him from Galilee, the Decapolis, Jerusalem, Judea, and from beyond the Jordan* (vv. 24-25).

AS WORD OF JESUS' HEALING POWERS SPREAD, thousands dropped everything and walked hundreds of miles to find him. Both those who would follow as disciples and those who followed to find healing would be given life in greater measure. Whether our motivation is self-giving or self-caring, it does not seem to matter to God. God will use any reason to welcome us, engage us, and to add to our lives.

God has given us a passion for life. The pursuit of healing motivates people to extreme measures. From all over the world those with resources travel to the Mayo Clinic and other centers of healing. Americans who can will seek out other parts of the globe in hopes that a treatment untested or prohibited in the United States might yield a miraculous cure. Billions are spent on medical research. People work hard to preserve the rain forest in the hope that some new medicine will be found there.

Had we lived two thousand years ago, we, too, would have pursued Jesus, seeking him out for ourselves or for those we love, to alleviate suffering, pain, and the absences of hope. It seems almost universal that in our suffering, we cry out to God in hopes of healing. If a miracle occurs, we thank God and our faith is thereafter strengthened. If a miracle does not happen, what then? A single mom spoke to me yesterday about her teenage daughter, who may not join the church with her. The teenager is angry at the church and at God. A year ago her best friend contracted a heart infection. After emergency treatment, surgeries, and many prayers, the friend seemed to be mending. Finally, a last restorative surgery that was assumed to be routine, ended surprisingly and tragically in death. A promising life was lost, and a best friend left devastated.

The inevitable question about God was asked: "Why did God let this happen?" The mother did her best to explain and comfort. But those who grieve deeply find the notion that "God has an unknown plan" to be small comfort at best and feeble theology at worst. So the teenager is choosing what may be the best restorative path left to her: to be angry at God and at the church. Far better to be angry than to let go of God altogether.

Ultimately each person encounters something that cannot be healed or fixed. We seek out Jesus. Sometimes we are healed in our body, our mind, our soul, or our relationships. Sometimes we are strengthened. Sometimes we doubt. We are left wondering how a loving God can allow tragedy and suffering to exist at all, especially when healing does not come. Still we come, drawn to one who also endured undeserved suffering and death. We realize that we are no different from any other living thing: we are a part of this cycle of life and death that God has made. Frustrated by our finitude, we have no choice but to yield ourselves into the hands of the One who made us in love. God reaches out to us in the mysterious places that are not illuminated by our logical minds. There God finds us. There God also gives us hope and new life.

———◆•◆•◆———

Consider Paul's words from Romans, and recall life experiences that speak to them: "We also boast in our sufferings, knowing that suffering produces endurance, and endurance produces character, and character produces hope, and hope does not disappoint us, because God's love has been poured into our hearts through the Holy Spirit that has been given to us" (5:3-5).

When all comfort seems absent, you are with me, God. Though I may sometimes feel alone, you never leave my side. When suffering and doubts come, grant me patience, endurance, and peace.

23

Week Two ~

Thursday: Never without God

Read Matthew 5:1-12. *"Blessed are the poor in spirit, for theirs is the kingdom of heaven"* (v. 3).

H AVE YOU EVER HEARD SOMEONE WONDER, "What have I done to deserve this?" or "Why would God let this happen to me?" or "Why is God punishing me?" Hearing these questions, have you been at a loss as to how to respond? Do you sense something wrong with their theology, but can't spell out why and wish you could? Read on.

When Jesus began his teaching with the words, "Blessed are you who . . . ," he is telling the people that God is with them. That God is with us may seem obvious, but people weren't so sure when Jesus walked the earth. Imagine the setting. Jesus has drawn the attention of enormous crowds, many who have traveled great distances to see, to hear, to be healed. Those who were in need of healing were living witnesses to a terrible understanding of God that was commonly held and taught. That teaching, simply put, goes like this: if you are obedient to God's laws, God is pleased and God rewards you. If you are disobedient to God's laws, God is displeased and God punishes you. If, therefore, life is treating you well, your family is intact, everyone is healthy, and you have abundant possessions and status, you must be leading a life of obedience to God's will, and God is rewarding you. If, however, you have a disease or any kind of a setback, or if you are poor or alone or persecuted, you must have done or are doing something wrong that is causing God to punish you.

Mixed into the crowd were also the religious authorities who followed Jesus. They, too, were wondering what Jesus was about. Some of them were hopeful that this might be the promised Messiah that would evict the Romans and lead Israel back to its status as a great nation. Their understanding of how this would come about involved a "repentance," by the whole nation, obeying God's laws so that God would reward the whole nation.

So what did Jesus have to say? "Blessed are the poor in spirit (or in Luke's Gospel, simply "the poor"), blessed are those who mourn, those who are persecuted." In other words, God is with you who are suffering: God has not abandoned you and is not punishing you. You have not necessarily done something wrong that bad things have happened to you. This was an enormous challenge to the theology that was being promoted by the religious establishment. From this moment on, an irreparable rift would grow between Jesus and the religious leaders. It was only a matter of time before they would use charges of heresy and blasphemy to silence and kill Jesus. The Word, once spoken, however, would not be silenced.

Imagine the joy, the relief, and the hope felt by so many who heard Jesus' words. To suffer as a natural consequence of a sinful act or a careless action is one thing, but to suffer as a victim of a random calamity or someone else's evil intent is much more difficult. Even worse is to have others assume that you have done something to deserve your suffering, that God is angry with you and punishing you, and that you deserve the accompanying judgment, ostracism, and shame.

"God is with you." This is not wishful thinking. This is not a dream of someday in the future. This is now. Your greatest advocate, the one who loves you most deeply, who treasures you as only one who gives birth to your being can, the one who believes in you when you have lost faith in yourself, that one stands with you at all times. This is a God to whom all our devotion can be given. This is a God to die for.

Jesus names God's Spirit as our advocate. What might God advocate for your life today?

My heart overflows with gratitude for your loving presence in my life, O God. May I, like a child, take your hand and follow where you would lead me. I give my life to you.

FRIDAY: THE WHOLE TRUTH

Read Matthew 5:13-20 *"Do not think that I have come to abolish the law or the prophets; I have come not to abolish but to fulfill them"* (v. 17).

WHEN MY FATHER DIED, we found some documents that would be helpful to my mother. Attached to the documents, Dad had written a summary of important information. At the conclusion of the business items were simple words to my mother saying that "love is too small a word" to express all that she meant to him and all he felt for her.

Love is too small a word. I don't imagine any word would be adequate, nor would any combination of words fully express a lifetime. So we leave it into the hands of one small word: love. Jesus, "the Word made flesh," made a crucial statement about God's presence in our lives in the Beatitudes. He followed it up with another grand claim for humans— telling us we are the salt and light of the earth. He pointed to himself as the fulfillment of all the law and the prophets. These immense ideas come in such quick succession that they may be missed unless replayed in slow motion.

Replay the words, "I have come to fulfill the law and the prophets." Now fast forward to Chapter 22, where Matthew spells out what this means in an important encounter between Jesus and a lawyer of the Pharisees and Sadducees. Asked what is the great commandment in the law, Jesus answered, "You shall love the Lord your God with all your heart, and with all your soul, and with all your mind. This is the great and first commandment. And a second is like it. You shall love your neighbor as yourself. On these two commandments depend all the law and the prophets." "All the law and the prophets" are built upon this pivotal foundation, this too small word, "love."

Jesus could have begun his teaching with a running list of all the things that were wrong with people, with society, with the church and its teachings. That's what I likely would have done at age thirty. A friend tells me that he and his debate partner in college almost always argued the negative side of a question. "It was always easier to show what was wrong with something than it was to come up with positive solutions."

In adolescence our insecurities lure us into being critical of everyone around us. As we age, that pattern may remain, taking on more sophisticated forms. But there is no life in it.

We may awaken from this cynicism when we realize that we've defined ourselves by what we are against, yet have little idea of what we are for. In Jesus we see one who knew what he stood for. We hunger to give ourselves to a greater cause, to find meaning for our life in a greater purpose. We join others on the mount where Jesus speaks, and listen carefully to his words.

People who encountered Jesus often commented that he was unlike their other teachers in that he spoke with authority. As we look at his life and teachings, we see that this simple little word, "love," was his center. All the law and the prophets were hinged on love. Love was his understanding of the heart of God. Love was the basis for his teachings— especially when he acted in contradiction to the teachings of others. Love meant his dying to self in order to be life-giving. Jesus was only against anything that was in contradiction to love. And Jesus calls us to hinge our whole life on this one little word, "love."

If the command of love is the hinge upon which all the law and the prophets rest, what are the implications of that for the way we read the rest of Scripture?

Sometimes I make my life so complicated, O God. Help me to slow down, to be focused on what is most important, and to live with love.

Saturday: The Game Played to Perfection

Read Matthew 5:21-44. *"You have heard that it was said, 'You shall love your neighbor and hate your enemy.' But I say to you, love your enemies and pray for those who persecute you"* (vv. 43-44).

My FATHER HAD A DELIBERATE PATTERN of playing card games. It worked well for "Hearts" and "Aw Shucks"—but my family also enjoyed a game we called "Pounce"—a kind of a communal solitaire that was won by intense speed. When we could persuade dad to join in, it added to the levity of the game to observe the contrast between the frantic pace engaged in by everyone, except dad. Like sitting in the eye of a hurricane, oblivious to the raging winds around him and uncaring about the possibility of winning, he would play at his usual deliberate pace—even at times pausing for a puff on his pipe. Most of us were disabled in our laughter over his style. He wasn't bothered by this—ours just wasn't a game he cared to be drawn into.

Jesus managed to be in the world, but not always driven by the world. He could play the game at his own pace and thus help us rethink our comfortable patterns. It is stunning how his teachings counter both the sacred teachings and the sacred writings of the church. As often happens, "the group" would not likely tolerate someone who walked to the beat of a different drummer. Not intimidated into toeing the party line, Jesus could and would, in the course of his life, challenge more than the six examples of teachings that he lifts up in this portion of the Sermon on the Mount. These six suffice to set the tone. The core of his life was settled—love God; love others; love self. Equipped with this starting point, this center from which everything else would follow, Jesus challenged the mistaken notions of those who thought they could obey the law and, with impunity, hate their neighbor, be lustful, divorce their spouse for spurious reasons, and get revenge on an enemy.

I am grateful for many who have, by their lives, reminded me that there are many ways to play the game of life that's dealt to us; those who have called me back to the core values of faith. I am grateful for my second cousin, born with Down's syndrome who lived his too-few years with unfailing love, faith, and joy, and thus reminded us of the qualities Jesus valued above all others. I am grateful for my mother who pursued strangers with warmth and hospitality. I am grateful for old Leonard who was unhampered by an I.Q. of 70, and modeled to my high school classmates and me a spirit of generosity as he would shovel the snow from his whole block, run errands for elderly neighbors, and delight us with his imaginative tales. I am grateful for my car mechanic who had few possessions, but was rich in friends. Each of us is able to choose the way we live our lives. As we listen to the teachings of Jesus and as we are guided by our faith, we may discover that at times we play our cards quite differently than at others.

The world's full of saints who remind us of the core values of our faith. When we drift into patterns, thoughts, and actions that are far from the ways of God, saints and prophets have a way of crossing our paths and calling us back to the core of who we are.

Love God. Love neighbor. Love self. Every act, every thought, every word, every moment, is an outgrowth of this core. This is what it is to "be perfect as your heavenly Father is perfect."

———•◆•———

Try to list the key values by which you live your life.

Thank you, Lord Jesus, for being a model of one who lived true to your beliefs and ideals. Help me to do the same.

Sunday: Praying the Bible

Read Matthew 6:1-18. *"And in praying, do not heap up empty phrases . . . for God knows what you need before you ask"* (v. 7).

I suppose many of us have had the experience of driving a car for a long time in a kind of stupor, only to "come to" and wonder how we managed to get from point A to point B. The same happens with a liturgy that's used over and over again; it's nice to know it by heart, but sometimes you have no memory of what you actually said.

My father also added a wrinkle to this phenomena. It was speed. As we would sit down for a meal together, we learned to pay attention to the body language if we wanted to join in the table grace. As his hands came together and his head lowered, we readied for the charge of "Come, Lord Jesus . . ." because if you didn't jump in as the starting gate opened, you'd never catch up. There was a sense of accomplishment if you came in a "tie" with the "Amen." We all assumed we knew what had been said to get to the end, but really didn't remember the particulars in getting there.

When people voice a desire for something different in worship, it often stems from an intuition that familiarity may not only breed contempt, but in the case of memorized spirituality, it can also breed "empty phrases" that have little meaning. The same can be said for hearing the same passages from the Bible. In a literate, fast-paced society, we are accustomed to reading as quickly as possible, and we develop a short-hand method of assimilating what is being read to us or what we are reading. All I have to do is to hear "Zacchaeus," for example, and in a flash, I mentally recall the whole story and my mind can tune out the details and go on to other things.

Once in a while, we are surprised when a word or a phrase jumps out from the rest, rises up from the mists of memory or the drone of repetition, speaks in a different way, and ceases to be a part of a heap of empty phrases. I have been surprised by the neglected phrase in Psalm 23, "He restoreth my soul" (v. 3). After forty years of knowing the words, I have been awakened by the implications of "how excellent is thy name in all the earth." I have been given hope to hear anew Jesus say, "Whoever has been forgiven little, loves little," because I knew the opposite to be true for me. These had been empty phrases until somehow my life tripped over them.

It is possible to read Scripture and to pray in ways that give a little more breathing room for the soul and for the Spirit of God to intercede. One such way is a method taught by the Benedictines for hundreds of years. Try it with today's reading—or with any of the day's readings—as you continue in your journey through Matthew.

Begin with a simple prayer that God's presence and wisdom might be experienced in your reading of today's text. Then begin reading: "Beware of practicing your piety before people in order to be seen by them" (Matt. 6:1). As you read, if something seems to catch your eye, if you feel drawn to a word or a phrase, stop your reading and begin the next phase of the process. Let us say, for example, there was something about "practicing piety before people in order to be seen" that hit you. Begin repeating that phrase over and over—out loud or silently. If it happens, let it condense itself to a few words, or even one word, as you repeat it. "Practicing piety before people in order to be seen . . . Practicing piety to be seen . . . Practicing piety." Allow yourself to take the word or words into yourself, as though you are swallowing them and making them a part of you by repeating them over and over.

When the repetition seems completed, end this phase and begin the third phase; the prayer. The prayer is a stream of consciousness dialogue with God. Thoughts may be brief or quite long. You will sense when enough is said. Then return to the Bible and resume the reading and the three-part cycle—reading, recitation, prayer. Part of the point of this method is to let go of the notion that you are in charge of understanding the text. Instead, let the Spirit of God speak through the reading and dialogue with your soul.

Write down the prayer that comes to you through the Benedictine method. Use journaling to expand on this exercise.

O God, thank you for speaking through Scripture. Thank you also for those who preserved the words of Jesus. May his words live truly in me.

Monday: The Tail that Wags the Dog

Read Matthew 6:19-24. *"For where your treasure is, there your heart will be also"* (v. 21).

To make a case for the concept of original sin, perhaps no better argument could be found than the simple word "mine." Once parents are through teaching their primacy through the mimicry of "mama" and "papa," a toddler takes very little time in reordering their notion of the cosmic hierarchy by asserting, "mine." Eventually, as faith in God grows, we come to realize there really isn't anything that's ours. Everything is God's. God honors us with the awareness that we are entrusted to be caretakers.

When I was a child, every Sunday's offering of money at our church concluded with the precise march of the ushers up the center aisle as we sang, "We give Thee but Thine own; what'er the gift may be. All that we have is Thine alone, a trust, O God, from Thee." In this way, we were reminded of true ownership and our stewardship of creation. It was a good reminder because our childhood voice is tempted to reassert itself, claiming, "Mine!" We sometimes grumble at how the church is always asking for "my" money, and subconsciously wanting to sing, "I give thee but Mine own; what'er the gift may be. All that I have is Mine alone, a gift, o God, to thee."

But deep inside, we know the words of Jesus ring true. We cannot serve God and money. It's one or the other. Which shall we give ourselves to? Even knowing the answer, it can prove to be very difficult to act on our knowledge. We know, where money is concerned, we are often like a drunk who says he or she can quit any day. It has always been a struggle. From the ancient myth of "the Midas touch" to its retelling in C.S.

Lewis' lake of gold in *The Dawn Treader*, from the lure of King Solomon's mines to the lottery's improbable odds, from folk proverbs of "money can't buy happiness" to "possession is nine-tenths of the law," we know the power of "mine." What should be the slave, easily becomes our master.

In the novel *Hanta Yo*, Ruth Beebe Hill describes the Plains Indians who defined their greatness not by how much they possessed, but by how much they were willing to give. It was a value based on placing the well-being of their tribe above individual well-being. The central character of the story demonstrated this value by giving everything away to the tribe and, following his total divestment, walking naked into the wilderness. In so doing, he demonstrated the truth of the tribe's belief.

If I claim the faith of Jesus, if I want to follow in his steps and be known as a Christian, the way I handle the tool of money is one of many disciplines that beckon me to "put my money where my mouth is." The church, in ancient wisdom, has always held to the concept of giving a minimum of ten percent of earnings away, as a way to practice what we believe, to help us keep God, and not money, as our master. A faith that has no implications for the practice of life is not a faith but a fairy tale. The words of Jesus may not be easy for those who hang onto the "mine" of adolescence, but their difficult honesty is a breath of fresh air for those who long to abide by God's truth.

<hr />

What does "Let your style of giving define your style of living" mean?

O God, may my faith be more than wishful thinking. May I have the courage to put the words of Jesus into practice. May my living the faith help me to grow in the faith.

Tuesday: The White Bear

Read Matthew 6:25-34. *"Do not worry about tomorrow. Today's trouble is enough for today"* (v. 34).

Freedom from worry is a rare thing. It is something we believe should be the birthright of every childhood. I was conscious of leaving this imagined state behind the day I left home for a summer job in California. Just a couple days after college graduation, soon to be married, driving my first car, it hit me: if anything goes wrong, I'm on my own. No parent to bail me out. The moment every teenager chafes for, now seemed a lonely spot. My worries have never disappeared.

Years later I found myself longing again to be the blissful child in the care of a parent. On the return home from a week in the Black Hills, our station wagon pulling a small trailer into the gathering darkness of night and a spring storm, my wife and I decided to find someplace in the South Dakota Badlands to tuck in and sleep through the storm. The problem is, in that barren land, places to tuck in are almost nonexistent. Tired and wanting to settle our four-year-old and seven-year-old sons for a night's sleep, we were relieved to see a sign for an overlook and pulled off the freeway. As we wound our way on a deserted gravel road, we were growing in our anxiety about things taking a turn for the worse. The rains had softened the volcanic gravel into a slippery quagmire. Our headlights disappeared into the driving rain. The tires had little traction, and we came sliding to a stop in the overlook's parking lot with a very bad feeling.

Rather than try to drive out, we did our best to settle in for the night. We carried our boys to the trailer, leaving our muddy shoes outside. They were oblivious to our worry, perched on some imagined precipice with the prairie winds howling. (The morning revealed it to be a real precipice.) Once everyone was tucked in for a night's sleep, I lay wide awake in the darkness, envious of our boys who innocently could trust that their well-being was taken care of by their parents. They didn't listen to the howling winds. They didn't feel the trailer rocking back and forth. They slept through the flash and crash of lightning all about. And they didn't wonder about being stranded, running-board-deep, in the middle of nowhere.

They had faith in us, and that was enough for them. In my heart, I knew theirs was the faith that I should have. I, as a child of God, should be able to rest in faith. But exhaustion, not faith, carried me into a fitful sleep. The next day brought sun, a drying wind, a firmer ground, a trip resumed, and a reminder of the beauty of a child's faith and the futility of worrying about tomorrow.

It's hard for us to follow Jesus' encouragement: Don't worry. We are like a person who, having agreed to be a part of a study, is placed in a room by themselves with these instructions: "You can think about anything you want in the next ten minutes while you're alone in this room, except that we don't want you to think about the white bear. If you do think about the white bear, however, please ring this bell every time you do." Of course, having been told to not think of the white bear drives each person to struggle to think of anything but the white bear.

We can't help it. We worry. Thoughts of the white bear will come, but Jesus gives some help to contain our worry. First, narrow worries down to what's immediately at hand. Let go of tomorrow. Focus on today's issues. That's enough.

Secondly, implied in this advice, is the wisdom that knows to sift out the concerns that we can do nothing about. They are like the issues of tomorrow and can be disposed of.

Once I have done what I can in the midst of the storms that rage, rather than lie wide-eyed awake, I can remember the words of Jesus. Consider the lilies, he advises us, or the birds, or a caterpillar, or anything that God has made and remember God in the midst of your storm. The worries may not disappear. The need to act on what you can will remain. But the lilies and the birds will remind us that we don't carry the weight of the world on our shoulders. There is only one God, and I am not the one. I am a child. I may no longer be blissfully ignorant, but I may be given peace for this day, and strengthened to live it well.

———◆———

Take a persistent worry. Name it. Apply Jesus' three-part advice to your concern. Act on what remains.

God grant me the courage to change the things that I can, the serenity to accept that which I cannot change, and the wisdom to know the difference. (Reinhold Neibuhr)

Wednesday: Follow the Drinking Gourd

Read Matthew 7:1-29. *"Everyone then who hears these words of mine and does them will be like those who are wise, who built their house upon the rock"* (v. 24).

> "This above all: to thine own self be true,
> And it must follow, as the night the day,
> Thou canst not then be false to any man.
> Farewell: my blessing season this in thee!"
> William Shakespeare, *Hamlet* (Act I, Scene 3)

My first reading of Shakespeare's *Hamlet* was forced upon me. I'm certain that, as with most assigned reading, I moved quickly through the text. I probably noticed bits and pieces of the advice Polonius gives his son Laertes, who is about to embark on an extended trip. They are excellent thoughts: "Give every man thy ear, but few thy voice . . . Neither a borrower nor a lender be . . . to thine own self be true . . ." In reading, I took them at face value.

When I first saw the play on stage, I was completely surprised. These gems of wisdom were presented as an endless list forced upon a son impatiently wanting to get on with the trip. The see-saw between the son taking a step to the boat and the father pulling him back for one more pearl of wisdom added a whole new dynamic to the words on a page. All the audience could relate to this experience, and the result was gales of laughter.

One wonders if Jesus sensed a growing restlessness in the crowd as the Sermon on the Mount nears its end. The pieces of his advice are briefer and hardly seem connected. Perhaps some eyes were glazing over and eyelids drooping. Knowing they need to wrap it up, a preacher or a parent musters one last image—an image that might carry itself beyond the sermon, beyond the lecture. Building a life upon a firm foundation and being true to one's self are the kinds of nuggets of wisdom that call us to the core of our being. We, who are created in the image of God, are called on to choose to live in ways that are true to our deepest nature, that are true to self. For those who are drawn to the truth of these words, there is no better example to show us what it means to live according to our true self than Jesus.

We who live in the northern hemisphere have always made use of an important star to help us find our way—the North Star. When I was a child, I was taught how to find this star. "Look for the Big Dipper, that group of seven stars that looks like a big cup with a long handle. Draw a line between the last two stars of the cup, the direction the liquid pours out, and keep going in that direction until you come to another bright star that stands alone. That's the North Star. No matter where you are or what time of night, the North Star is always straight north." One hundred and fifty years ago, slaves escaping into freedom in North America called the dipper the "drinking gourd," and they sang about how following the "drinking gourd" would "carry you to freedom."

Jesus is the star we follow, the star that guides us to freedom and keeps us from becoming lost. Even Jesus could not give a gem of advice for each aspect of our lives—neither then nor in our more complicated time. So he concludes the Sermon on the Mount with the image of building our house upon a rock instead of sand. Jesus promises that insofar as we live our lives centered on God's love and his teachings, we will be able to withstand the difficulties and storms that life will bring.

———◆◆◈◆◆———

What is the most important piece of advice someone has given you? In what ways is their advice consistent with your true self?

O God of all creation, the wellspring of love, we thank and praise you for giving us Jesus to know and follow. May we build our lives so firmly on you that, when storms come, we find ourselves held firmly in your loving care.

Week Three　⌐

Thursday: To Be of Use

Read Matthew 8:1-17. *"Truly I tell you, in no one in Israel have I found such faith"* (v. 10).

A WEEK IN THE WOODS CHANGES YOUR PERSPECTIVE. I don't mean the woods at a retreat center, nor the woods in a campground with RVs, cars, picnic tables, and tents in close proximity. I mean the deep woods where a person has only a very few of the comforts of civilization to support an adventure into places far from roads, houses, and power lines. I mean places that have only what you can carry, where you are by yourself, or with only a few others to share the primitive beauty. Radios and cell phones are left behind. The silence is deep. The smells are pure and sweet. The sun is the only reminder of time. Immersed in the change of surroundings, one hardly thinks of what was left behind.

Sooner or later the adventurer comes out of the woods. As we reenter "civilization," everything is loud, the pavement seems hard and unnatural, buildings are angular, their colors garish, the smells are harsh, and the sun glares instead of beaming with delight. Though a cleansing hot shower and a chilly drink hissing on ice are wonderful, they do not erase a desire to run back to the woods.

open arms that do not always first insist upon a confession of guilt.

Jesus saw a paralytic. Without knowing anything about him other than what he saw, and before anyone said a word, Jesus said simply, "Take heart, son; your sins are forgiven." This was a challenge to the dominant theology of the day that believed a physical malady such as paralysis was God's direct punishment for sin. The reaction of the teachers of the law indicates that Jesus was aware of what he was doing when he said, "Your sins are forgiven." Jesus meant, "God is not angry with you. God is not punishing you by inflicting you with paralysis. Though your body is not whole, you are restored to wholeness with God. Take heart. God is not vindictive, but loving. God welcomes you to pour out the troubles of your soul."

Imagine if we fully trusted these words of Jesus. We could begin a church service with words like these: "Our loving God, from whom no secrets are hid, forgives you freely and fully of all your sins. God invites you to pour out the troubles of your soul, to walk in paths of beauty and balance once again, and to take heart." Then some time for confession and a sign of peace would come. Imagine if we fully trusted Jesus' images of a loving parent, reaching out to the prodigal with open arms, instead of leading with the picture of the vice-principal leafing unhappily through our files. Imagine what it might mean to take away any reason for the child to respond with belligerence, twisting anger's logic into a defense of sin.

Another more subtle and sinister force was unsettled by Jesus' words and actions in this story. The teachers of the law were more interested in preserving their order than seeing someone restored to health. Unhealthy patterns resist change. A whole town begged Jesus to stay away, lest any more swine would be lost because someone was freed from demons. A family takes a misbehaving child to a therapist hoping for a quick fix, and the therapist surprises the family with the notion that the whole family has unhealthy patterns that it resists changing while sacrificing one of its own. Someone who is abused believes the abuser's lie that it's the victim's fault. A juvenile in trouble with the law objects to the unfairness of it all.

Jesus doesn't try to convince us of our sin. He just refers to it as a matter of fact: "your sins." No secrets are hidden from God. Absolutely none. There is no chance for denial or scapegoating or rationalizing. We may as well be honest. But take heart. Be encouraged and have courage, because old patterns will fight to keep their place. Your old friends will no longer carry you. Say goodbye to your appetite for possessions and status. It will be enough and everything to hear Jesus give voice to God's word, "Take heart, son. Take heart, daughter. You are home. Find the way to and from here."

⬦

Where have you experienced grace that has given you courage to redress wrongs and change old patterns?

Thank you, God, for calling me to confession. I know you will not punish me, but restore me to health.

Saturday: Letting Go to Follow Jesus

Read Matthew 9:9-17. *"Go and learn what this means: 'I desire mercy, and not sacrifice'"* (v. 13).

I'm sitting in a coffee shop in a bookstore. Tables are close; everyone is full. It's easy to eavesdrop, if I want. Mini-stories unfold. A cell-phone message is spoken as though everyone wanted to hear, and I am annoyed. A daughter teases a five-minute-late mother, and I am amused. The parade naturally marches by, as though for my entertainment, while I am able to stay in place. I enjoy people-watching, but I fight my inclination to draw conclusions and pass judgment on the scenes around me. It is easy to remain aloof and detached, as though I am in some movie theater. It is a mind game that keeps me at a distance. I do not like it when I do it.

I do not like the mind game of being an outside observer because I can do the same thing in a different way. The same dynamic can happen as I review today's reading. I observe Jesus eating with the outcast of his community. I watch the moralists stand in judgment. I look at the several insightful sayings of Jesus and keep my safe distance by treating them in an intellectual way. I know, however, the words of Jesus were not recorded to be studied from a distance, but to be lived.

The power of Jesus' words and actions, his dynamic spirit refuses to remain in the past. When my life is painful, when I'm lost and out of balance, when darkness gathers, I hear the words of Jesus, "I come for those in need of a physician," and I take heart. Christ is in the midst of my life and never more present than at my points of need. He gives strength for the weary, comfort for the suffering, and hope in the dark nights.

I take these thoughts with me as I leave my table to get a refill on my cup of coffee. Now I begin to look around me—not as the one in charge of the thoughts, but as one who is listening to the words in Matthew's Gospel. I see how I take the role of the Pharisees, standing in judgment of those around me. It is I who Jesus is talking about; I am in need of a physician. I am not apart from or above those around me. When I discover I am being critical of others, it is often true that I am not happy inside myself. Something is out of balance and in need of healing.

I reread the words from Matthew, "Go and learn what this means," and I think to myself, "How can I presume to write about this when I can be such a Pharisee? Who am I to think I might have something to say about this?" I don't have anything to say, really, except that I know I need to hear the words of Jesus. I am in need of a physician. I require mercy.

As these thoughts spin, I look around the shop from my table. The scene remains the same. My place in it is altered. I'm off my high horse, and I am among others. These are my brothers and sisters given by God. We are all in need of a physician, at times. And we could all do with a place of welcome.

There is another who is present in this coffee shop and I am beginning to see him. Lord Jesus is here just as he sat at the table with everyone so long ago. All are welcome in his presence. Grace calls us to let down our guard, see ourselves as we are, and bask in the love of God and in the fellowship of God's family.

Have you found a connection between being more at peace with your own shortcomings and your ability to be more graceful with others?

Thank you, God, for treating me with mercy, for your healing, and for the joy of being well in mind and soul. Help me let go of my judgment of others.

Sunday: Pray for Laborers

Read Matthew 9:18-38. *When he saw the crowds, he had compassion on them* (v. 36).

As I walk down the long, clean corridor of the post surgical wing, I am barely noticed in the bustle surrounding me. The staff at the unit's desk are engrossed in their tasks. A nurse with a cart full of meds is making her rounds. Open doors reveal a variety of activity—from catnaps and family company, to quick exams and expectant looks. But no one calls for me in this hospital.

It was different in the nursing home I just left. In most nursing homes, residents look expectantly, hoping to see a face they recognize. If they no longer recognize faces, they still look, hoping to be recognized. Some cry out incessantly. There always seem to be a few making their rounds to friends less mobile. They hold onto the side rails or slowly wheel their chairs on their errands of mercy.

After years of visiting people in hospitals and nursing homes, I have yet to get used to these scenes and have not become immune to feelings that stir. Where do all these people come from? How can so many be experiencing illness or frailty in their old age? And I give thanks for the many angels of mercy that work here, day in and day out. I pray for God's presence, because I feel inadequate and overwhelmed by the needs that surround me. I go about my business—a visit or two, devotions for a chapel service. Then I slip out, often with a prayer of gratitude that I can leave, and a prayer asking forgiveness, because at times I'm glad to be free of the press of others' needs around me.

How did Jesus do it? People pressed around him, calling on him for help, pulling at him, competing for his time. Still he looked with compassion on the masses. He knew their needs were great. And he knew he was only one man. So he told his disciples to pray for laborers. And this prayer reaches out to each one who reads it.

Jesus didn't ask for someone to save the whole world. Instead, he used a simple image—a harvest, which in those days was done by hand. One bunch of grapes at a time. One ear of corn. One olive after another. Painstaking and steadfast. Bit by bit until it adds up to a whole harvest. These are the deeds of mercy and compassion Jesus calls for.

When Einstein was once asked what he thought was the greatest invention of modern man, he replied whimsically, "compound interest." He knew the power of adding a little bit each day and how that builds over time. Deeds of mercy compound daily. I think of Ruby, nearly blind but still able to knit hats and scarves and mittens, gathering others around weekly at her house to do the same. Fingers move from memory, creating gifts of love to go to homeless people, to refugee people, to poor people. These gifts lift hearts and build bridges across the world.

I think of Marge, so deaf she can barely hear church services, even with hearing aids. But her friendly smile brightens hearts. She is among those making blankets to send around the globe. Every month she sits in the church basement at her sewing machine, finishing the borders of those blankets.

The interest in compassion compounds. I am only one, but I am one among many.

Who was the "least of these" that you encountered today? What happened?

Dear Jesus, strengthen me for the day to come, that your healing touch may be given through me.

Monday: Finding the Way

Read Matthew 10:1—11:1. *"I am sending you out like sheep among wolves. Therefore be as shrewd as snakes and as innocent as doves"* (v. 16).

DO YOU REMEMBER AN OLD CAMP SONG that begins, "Children go where I send thee. How shall I send thee?" The question that's answered deals with "how," not "where" or "what attainable and measurable results will we report upon our return." That's very close to the essence of what we know of the mission of Jesus' disciples in the tenth chapter of Matthew. It also gives us an important lesson about living our Christian faith today.

When my oldest son was in second grade, he was driven to rush through his math workbooks. He was amazingly goal-oriented. Getting to the end was his focus, and his mother and I didn't think the process of getting there seemed much fun for him. When his younger brother entered scouting, we saw the same dynamic. Ranks and badges were earned quickly. The list of requirements to earn each one seemed to be obstacles to get past rather than opportunities to broaden his knowledge and experience.

I know where my sons picked up this value of pushing for a goal's completion. But I have come to believe that reaching a goal should not be the dominant style or philosophy of life. When I see a television advertisement praise a couple's ability to travel and thus be able to "check number six off their life goal's list," something inside me twists uncomfortably. That seems wrong. Shouldn't my highest value for life be how I travel—the way I live my life—more than where I am going or whether or not I ever arrive?

Jesus has impacted my approach to life. The early Christian Church was sometimes referred to as "The Followers of The Way," or simply "The Way." We follow Jesus who spoke of himself as being "the way, the truth, and the life." Ours is a commitment to ordering our daily life according to the path of love. Our ethics reflect this commitment and are summarized by this classic statement: "The end does not justify the means. It is the means that justifies the end." It is more important for Christians who follow "the way," to be loving as we work toward goals and dreams, than it is to arrive at certain end results. The Apostle Paul writes of this same wisdom: "If I have all faith, so as to remove mountains, but have not love, I am nothing" (I Cor. 13:2).

This is not to say that we set aside goals and objectives, or that we don't work for good results. But we recognize that difficulties arise if we are dominated by attaining certain goals. What happens if I don't get the grade I worked for or gain entry into a certain school or work program? What if a goal is attained but begins to crumble—a job is lost, or a relationship falls apart? If I have structured my life around the need to achieve end results to justify my being, do these setbacks devastate me with the thought of being a failure? And if I check everything off my life goal list, but have done so without being guided by love, what's the point?

Jesus sent the disciples out with the commission to announce the presence of God's realm and to "Heal the sick, raise the dead, cleanse lepers, cast out demons" (Matt. 10:8). The game plan was to love those where there was need. He warned them that not everyone would welcome them. They couldn't expect that they could force their agenda on everyone. The principle of love would show them how they would proceed.

As we make following Jesus in the path of love our dominant motivation, we discover that our life goals are shaped by the process of following. What we set out to accomplish may change. We may discover that one goal needs to be replaced with another. We may even achieve far greater and different summits than we set our sights on in the first place. Whatever the result, we know that following Jesus in the path of love can help us handle adversity and failure, brings joy in the process, and allows a deep sense of peace in the end.

When has the path of love caused you to change or let go of a goal?

Dear God, as I live my life help me to shape my days with an awareness of my desire to follow your will and your path of love.

Tuesday: Blind Sighted

Read Matthew 11:2-26. *"Go and tell John what you hear and see: the blind receive sight. . . . Let anyone with ears listen!"* (vv. 4, 15).

As a part of a wilderness survival school, my son and I were among a dozen people on a walk along fields and into wooded paths, learning more about wild edible plants. The July air was still, hot, and humid. The foliage overhead was thick, a mottled spectrum of greens, offering refuge from the intense sunshine. Our attention was focused on the path, on each other, and on the specimens being identified and gathered. Unknown to us, staff volunteers had gone ahead and were hidden on our route. One had caked every inch of his mostly naked body with mud and leaves. He had climbed a tree and was comfortably hugging its trunk, invisible to us who passed ten feet below. Once we passed, he wildly shook the tree limbs to gain our attention. We laughed at how blind we had been. Another volunteer furrowed himself into a muddy, grassy gully near where we walked. Some even stepped on his outstretched arm, and unknowingly walked by. Again, with our passing, he moaned loudly enough that our eyes were opened to what we had seen.

John the Baptist had to overcome tunnel vision in order not to be blind to what he was seeing. In *A Life of Jesus*, Shusaku Endo writes of how John's image of God was quite different from that of Jesus: "The image of God that John embraced was a father-image—the image of a grim, censorious deity." Unlike John, Endo writes, Jesus' "heart was like a maternal womb to engender an image of God which more closely resembles a gentle mother, the image of God which he would disclose to the people on a mountain by the Lake of Galilee."

John looked for what he expected to see, and had to overcome preconceptions to see the truth before his very eyes. "Go and tell John what you hear and see," Jesus told John's emissaries. Then he went on to talk about John being "the Elijah who was to come," and if they were able to consider this without tunnel vision, they might be able to see it. In the same vein, he spoke of Korazin and Bethsaida, towns that witnessed Jesus' miracles but remained blind. No amount of shaking the limbs or moaning at their feet was able to jog them out of their entrenched ways. What will do it for us?

Hunters know that all animals have their blind spots. When not on guard, all creatures walk with tunnel vision. This is why deer hunters build stands and find ways to put a platform up in a tree. Even when something in our daily environment changes, we can have a hard time seeing it. A friend shaves his beard, and we have this low-level feeling that something is different. It may not hit us for days. In our daily routines, in our hectic lives, and in our insulated habits, we become numb and blind to the realities before our eyes. Relationships flat-line, thinking petrifies, and passions grow cold.

If you're like me, you have moments when you don't feel alive to the life that's around and within you. Maybe you, too, have an intuition that the routine and safe assumptions carry with them the danger of close-mindedness and boredom. I find hope in the possibility that I can awaken to new life.

It's no accident that Jesus follows his observations in response to John, along with his harsh words about Korazin and Bethsaida, with a simple prayer of praise that God has "hidden these things from the wise and learned, and revealed them to little children." Little children engage the world with eyes wide open and hearts full of joy. Little children hear the stories about Jesus, which are brand-new and fresh. Their imaginations have room for the spirit's growth, and their hearts hunger for God's loving embrace. I know there's a child within each of us. God begins each one of us that way. And God never stops claiming us as sons and daughters, children of God.

Marcus Borg has written a book entitled *Meeting Jesus Again for the First Time*. What do you imagine this might mean for you?

May I remember, O God, that each day is brand new, a blank page to write the story of my life. May I fill my days with words of love and deeds of compassion.

WEDNESDAY: TRUE LOVE

Read Matthew 11:25-30. *"Come to me, all you that are weary and are carrying heavy burdens, and I will give you rest. Take my yoke upon you, and learn from me; for I am gentle and humble in heart, and you will find rest for your souls"* (vv. 28-29).

WITH OPEN ARMS, God calls us home. Seeing everything about us—our gifts and failings, our triumphs and disappointments, our hopes and discouragements, our trust and betrayals, our power and weaknesses, our goodness and our evil—divine love longs to gather us in. Love longs to be one with the beloved. Time or distance or events do not diminish the power of true love. And God loves us truly.

Jesus speaks words each of us longs to hear, "Come to me." There is a place of loneliness within each human heart.

Sometimes the lonely place is felt when we are unsupported or when our cares are unknown by others. Sometimes the lonely place is where no one seems to understand or care for the thoughts and feelings closest to our hearts. A lonely place may harbor sad memories, or it may take the shape of fears for tomorrow. Our isolation in such places can become so intense that we seem unable to escape it.

In the silence of our lonely places, Jesus' deep words of love call us from isolation. More than that, God's heart of love melts the walls that keep us alone. More than just hearing the words of Jesus calling us to come, we feel his deep love, and our hearts leap for joy. We are not alone. We are held by the greatest and most complete love.

The release we feel as we give ourselves to God's love gives deep peace. A child scrapes her knee on a fall. Rising with a quivering lip, she runs home. The struggle to contain her tears ends the moment the gentle arms of her mother or father lifts her. In the safety of love, her tears and sobs can flow. Finally, she is not alone in her pain. A parent's love feels her pain, and the child knows the parent hurts for her. Healing begins with knowing she is not alone. The burden is shared. The load is lightened.

Jesus takes each one of us into love's embrace. We are not alone. God feels our heart and shares our burden.

I once gave a confirmation class a meditation exercise: in short, imagine an encounter with God and what is said in such an encounter. A seventh-grade girl, her first experience with guided meditation, recounted her encounter. She saw herself in a horse corral. She felt safe. It was there God met her, held her at arm's length while looking deeply into her eyes. "It will be okay," is all God said. She knew what God was talking about and it meant everything to her at that moment. In two days she was to meet her biological father for the first time. Little had been said about him in her younger years. Now that he had settled from a troubled past, he was reaching out to her. Her mother and stepfather were helpful in letting this piece of her past come into focus. The prospect had been a jumble of curiosity, fear, and hope. Now she knew that God was with her and that all would be well. The burden had been shared and Christ's yoke was on her shoulders. She was not alone.

Coming home to God does not mean we avoid the world. We might manage that only if we avoid God. God's embrace will not deflect the hurts, the challenges, the responsibilities, and the need to act. Quite the opposite. God's embrace strengthens us for action, clarifies how we are to be, and inspires us to give of the compassion we have received.

There is still a yoke that is placed on our shoulders. But look! It is not a yoke for one, but for two. This is the yoke of Christ who pulls with us every step of the way. True love walks with us. Always.

Take some time, with eyes closed and mind settled, to imagine an encounter with God.

Thank you, Lord Jesus, for holding me with love and giving strength for my journey.

Week Four ~

Thursday: What We Worship

Read Matthew 12:1-21. *"Something greater than the temple is here"* (v. 6).

ANY TIME OUR TREATMENT OF CHRISTIAN DOCTRINE adversely affects the way we treat each other, we have a problem. Jesus challenged the doctrines regarding the Sabbath because they were getting in the way of acts of compassion. The same reversal of priorities persists to this day, with the events that unfold in the land where Jesus walked feeling doubly tragic. We know that something is terribly wrong when people fight and kill each other because they deem certain sites to be so holy as to warrant disregarding the commandment against killing. We remember Jesus' words and know that the spirit of Christ continues to cry out for "justice to the nations." It is sad enough when people inflict pain on one another, but it is more so when the wounding is done with holy pretense.

Unholy acts in God's name are not limited to distant times and lands. They come in events both big and small, blatant and subtle. My dear friend Percy, one of the most holy people I've known because of his deeds of compassion and kindness through his "ministry" as an auto mechanic, finally told one of his own adult children to stop pestering him about religion and his lack of church attendance. The combat is played out by any one of us who presumes to know the mind and heart of God and therefore has a right to inflict our standards on others under the guise of moral superiority. A trail of damage follows in the wake of righteous causes: those denied access to Holy Communion pending doctrinal correctness, those having to justify their divorces to religious authority before rebuilding their lives, those honest enough to raise questions in the face of doctrinal arrogance, or schisms that damage innocent generations to come, for example. There are so many times we need to remember Jesus' words: "Go and learn what this means, 'I desire mercy, not sacrifice'" (Matt. 12:7).

Like a lone great horned owl roosting in a tall pine, Jesus attracted the attention of the religious establishment—crows who circled around him, squawking their complaint, dive-bombing with questions, and plotting his demise. It is easy for me to join the crows. I am a part of the religious establishment, after all. It's my job to protect the sanctity of the sabbath and to promote the well-being of the church. I could justify all my time and energy being given to this task; meanwhile the cries of the lame go unheeded and the livestock flounder in the ditch.

Bishop Hanns Lilje of Germany, visiting the St. Paul, Minnesota, Luther Theological Seminary faculty in the early 1960s, was asked his opinion about the literal interpretation of the Bible, a heated issue at the time. People were arguing about the "historical-critical" methods of biblical interpretation. A great deal of energy was expended on the question, which became a flash-point for many congregations. Bishop Lilje said that the issue reminded him of being on a ship that could barely move because some of the crew were always in the water, looking for holes in the ship's hull. He quoted Jesus, saying "O ye of little faith," reminding those gathered that the church has great tasks and should not become dead in the water while guarding the ship's seaworthiness.

There are so many important issues facing our world today. They are unparalleled in their critical nature for the survival of our planet. Jesus calls us to the priorities of compassion. This may remain clear to us if we remember to worship God and not the sabbath, if we remember that God desires mercy over judgment.

<hr />

Try writing down the ten things you think God is most concerned with—four for the world, three for your community, and three for your family and friends.

Dear God, help me from being judgmental of others. May I look first to see their good and speak quickly to be affirming of those you have placed in my life.

Friday: I Don't Understand

Read Matthew 12:22-50. *"For out of the abundance of the heart, the mouth speaks"* (v. 34).

"Why do we need to take Communion, Dad? I mean, if we simply ask God for forgiveness and believe it's granted, then we don't need to have Communion, right?"

These were the kind of questions I sometimes asked my father. It is the inherent role of every teenager to challenge the beliefs of their parents—behind their backs, or with frontal attacks, or both. I would sometimes sit in the overstuffed chair in dad's study (the same chair I sit in now thirty-five years later, reminiscing). His desk lamp was the lone light. His pipe smoke swirled above the bowl with each puff, drifting into the room's smog. He would lean back and lazily chew on my questions before responding. It was as though he was back in college or grad school, back in the endless debates of philosophy. It seemed that I could never ruffle his feathers or get his goat with intellectual debate. What I thought were clever questions usually seemed to be ones he had asked himself. It wasn't gratifying for a teenager wanting a fight.

"I suppose you're right," he said. "You don't need to have Communion for God's forgiveness." Well, I got that one right, but I was a little disappointed that I didn't get more of an argument. Eventually I came to realize that my father was perfectly comfortable with a faith that didn't need to understand everything. He enjoyed the questions as frontiers that held the possibility of new discovery.

Even the brightest or most self-assured biblical scholars will admit that they do not understand everything in the Bible. We are finite humans, unable to apprehend the infinite being of God. Yet God seems eager to help us do the best we can.

There are several parts of what Jesus has to say in today's reading that I do not understand. What he has to say about a "house divided" makes sense. It's a good rebuttal to those who arrogantly attack him. But then along come these puzzling comments about forgiveness: People will forgive anything, but blasphemy against the Holy Spirit is unforgivable. What is blasphemy against the Holy Spirit? I do know that this verse has been used by people and the church in different ages who presume to know and who have used their supposed knowledge in cruel ways. But I don't understand it. Moreover, I don't know what Jesus means with his reference to the queen of the south who will come with judgment for their generation. And I don't like his treatment of his mother and brothers.

Further study might give me some additional information and insight. Often such pursuits are beneficial and can yield unexpected results. However, I do not always choose to read Scripture with the goal of unraveling every question that I encounter. More often than not, I read the words of Jesus knowing that I will find something that will be helpful, something that had been passed by unnoticed in prior readings that new catches my eye.

How sad it must have been for Jesus to perform amazing and beautiful works of compassion, only to have his motives questioned and slandered. If I were in his shoes, I can imagine feeling sadness and anger over their petty response to compassionate healings. In the midst of his response comes this little sentence: "For out of the abundance of the heart, the mouth speaks" (Matt. 12:34). Now that's something I find important to consider and understand.

———◆◆◆———

What unresolved questions about faith or the Bible do you have? Which of these are troubling and which ones no longer disturb you?

Dear God, I thank you for mystery in my life; for the things that I don't seem to understand, but that cause awe, joy, and gratitude to you.

Saturday: A Story for Today

Read Matthew 13. *He told them many things in parables* (v. 3).

When "once upon a time . . ." is spoken, everyone becomes a child again. Our attention focuses not so much on the speaker as on what might come next. A story is about to be told. We all love a story.

The thirteenth chapter of Matthew is filled with stories. Some of them are only two sentences long. Each of them could begin, "Once upon a time." Jesus knew the power of stories. He used them often to express important truths about God and ourselves. A story gives us permission to enter, to add our own thoughts, to identify and feel, and to learn about ourselves without being forced. Libraries, bookstores, television, theaters, and video stores all demonstrate that we have a voracious appetite for stories.

Both my sons loved a certain story when they were small children. As they were snuggled in bed and I would lie down beside them, I would sometimes remember to begin my story like this: "Once upon a time, there were two boys named Joel and Stephen." They would always chuckle, delighted to have their story told. The story that followed was simply a telling of what they did that day. If I missed something, they would fill it in. And if it wasn't long enough, they'd be quick to ask, "What else?" There wasn't a great deal in their young lives that would seem of significance to anyone else. But it was their day and their lives. Telling their story meant they were significant. They knew it and reveled in it.

Sometimes I end my day and can hardly remember anything I've done, let alone remember anything that's worthy of a story. As this day's evening nears, I take a moment to think of what I've done. I encouraged a person on the mend from heart bypass surgery. I shared laughter with co-workers. I held my wife's hand. I cheered four teens in their cross-country skiing race. I spoke with both sons on the phone, helping them resolve a sticky issue. I took my dog to the store for some dog bones. None of this seems worthy of a story. Still, it is my life, and that's significant. As I look back on this day I think, "Well, I've been a cheerleader today. I feel good about that. There may be other days that my story doesn't read so well or amount to much. Not today. This is worth a 'Once upon a time, there was a boy named Andrew . . .'"

Jesus was constantly encouraging others, pulling for everyone within earshot, even the ones he yelled at. His stories draw out the best in people: Be the seed in good soil. Be those who hear and who understand with their hearts. Be the mustard seed, the treasure hunter, the merchant, the good fish, and the good seed. He calls us into our story.

Jesus never seemed discouraged about a person's past. He was gracious to people in the present. And he was always hopeful for their future. If our God meets us, must we not also give ourselves the same spirit that God shows us? There is nothing in our past that God cannot help us with and use for good. There is nothing about today that is beyond God's grace. And with God in our story, who knows what tomorrow might bring?

———◆·◆·◆———

". . . tomorrow is a new day with no mistakes in it," Lucy Maud Montgomery's Anne of Green Gables tells us in another story. What was written on the blank page of your life's story today?

Dear God, thank you for honoring the days of my life by being in my story. May the story of my today give you joy in its telling.

Sunday: Stop

Read Matthew 14. *Then he ordered the crowds to sit down on the grass* (v. 19).

Suppose you find yourself lost in the woods. What things would you take care of and in what order? Remember, there are four different needs that can result in your death if you don't take care of them. Try to name them, beginning with the least important. Take a moment before reading further to name them to yourself.

How did you do? Most groups can put their heads together and come up with them. Food is the least important of the four. We can go a good month without food. Eventually, of course, our body needs fuel. Water—good drinkable water—is the third most important issue. We can go only a few days without water. The second most important issue is staying warm. Hypothermia can kill us within a matter of hours. Most important of all—what can get us into trouble more quickly than body warmth, water, or food, is panic. When a person panics, actions can be foolish and dangerous, causing our situation to deteriorate very rapidly. So the first step is to sit down: stop and settle yourself.

When life throws you a curve, when something goes wrong and you are faced with a crisis, what are the most important steps to take and in what order? With the lessons of wilderness survival as a background, it is more apparent that we may all too often neglect an important step. Before any other response, a quick or a long prayer—even a deep breath calling on God's wisdom and strength—is the first and most important step. The tasks ahead may not come easily, but knowing God is present settles us for actions that follow and that will help set our course.

In Matthew's fourteenth chapter, we read about three crisis moments and three different results. The first concerns Herod, the political leader of his people, who does not want to deal with the pressure applied by John regarding his own morality. Because Herod ignored this fundamental principle of turning to God, his actions, already bad, became even worse.

Then there are the disciples who are stressed out because there are so many people who hang around, and there's no way to help them with their needs. "Send them away," they decide, before consulting with Jesus. Perhaps we do the same on any issue when we look to God—not first for advice and guidance, but second—for endorsement of a previous action and aid with what we decide we want to have happen.

Finally, the wind picked up, buffeting their ship in the night. Jesus walked to them on the water. Not only were they not calling on God, their panic seemed to increase when they saw Jesus. So it is that we, knowing that God's presence might call upon us in a way we don't want, may find ourselves turning our back on God. "It's a ghost." "It's only the memory of my childhood lessons I have since rejected." "It's old-fashioned." "None of my friends operate that way." "I am only one person, and I wouldn't make a difference anyway." But if we stop and turn to Jesus, he comes to us when our life is buffeted and can help us walk in godly paths.

Our Departments of Natural Resources have an acronym they teach people entering the woods. If you think you are lost or are in trouble, STOP: Sit. Think. Observe. Plan. They know it is important not to panic, but to draw on the best resources available. In faith we act on this wisdom. In trouble or as a matter of daily rhythm, we stop, pray, listen, and follow God.

———◆◆◆———

What is causing you stress? Take a moment to walk this troubled water in your mind to the outstretched hand of Jesus. What is the help he gives?

O God, may I sense your calming presence, your strengthening hand, and your guidance this day.

Monday: What Rules?

Read Matthew 15:1-31. *Great crowds came to him, bringing with them the lame, the maimed, the blind, the mute, and many others* (v. 30).

I HAVE A FRIEND WHO DOESN'T COLOR INSIDE THE LINES. She drives a VW mini-bus. Using bright yellow contact paper, she decorated its flat front with a brilliant rising sun. The back of the van is covered with bumper stickers. Her artistic enterprises are varied—from stick houses and furniture to jewelry made with laundry lint. Her children are given room to be free spirits. The last time we were at their house, my wife had to dodge one who was circling the inside on in-line skates. She appeals to the part of me that does not want to be boxed in by anyone else's norm.

I don't mind convention and tradition. However, I often am irritated when I feel pressure to conform. I would never make it in a community that has rules for the kind of mail-boxes and the colors of house trim or roofs and where dandelions were frowned upon. So I find myself drawn to those moments when Jesus took on the Pharisees and challenged rules that made little sense.

Jesus challenged those who insisted on conforming to a tradition. It's not that washing hands before eating isn't a good idea. It still is! Jesus' real objection had to do with rules that had become more important than caring for others. The Pharisees went their way, grumbling about Jesus' rejection. The disciples reported how the Pharisees were offended. That's another pattern often used when social pressures are applied. Use a triangulation of communication. Make snide comments about your neighbor. Hope that someone passes on the comments: "People are saying that . . ." "A few have told me that . . ." "The way we've always done that is . . ."

Churches are filled with traditions. Even when the traditions have value, it may be wise to hold them loosely so we remember what is the heart of our life together. When I did a year's interim as pastor of an older, traditional parish, a part of my job was to help prepare them for changes that would inevitably come with a new pastor. There were some who knew that changes could be a healthy part of their renewal. I began to randomly make some changes—a kind of "tweaking" the system to see what would happen. I omitted the confession they were used to from the liturgy and was soon told by one that she wanted it back—especially on Sundays with communion. We had a brief conversation about the theological rationale. I thanked her for coming directly to me with her concern, because more than the issue itself, I was concerned about how communication regarding traditions would be handled. Traditions must not become the rule, but must be ruled by love.

The Canaanite woman broke with tradition. She spoke to a Jewish man in public. For the sake of her daughter's well-being, guided by love, she ignored a taboo. Jesus broke his society's norm by being willing to address her. Healing comes by the rule of love.

———•◦◦•———

When have you found tradition interfering with the path of love? Which traditions are helpful to your faith life?

Lord Jesus, thank you for your life among us and showing us the path of love.

Tuesday: An Honest Look

Read Matthew 15:32—16:12. *"How could you fail to perceive that I was not speaking about bread? Beware of the yeast of the Pharisees and Sadducees!" Then they understood . . .* (v. 16:11).

Again and again Jesus' disciples asked him to interpret his parables. Then, when Jesus used a simple metaphor, "the yeast of the Pharisees and Sadducees," they took him literally and wondered whose bread they should avoid in the marketplace. You can imagine Jesus rolling his eyes at the dull-wittedness of his select group. How would it ever be possible that his work and message would be sustained if handed over to such dim bulbs? The Pharisees and Sadducees seemed to get the point quicker than the disciples.

I'm surprised that the Gospels so often depict the disciples in an unflattering light. They don't understand Jesus' teachings. They try to fend off those they deem unimportant—often women and children. They argue about who's the greatest and jostle for access to power. They abandon Jesus. Yet they include their blatant shortcomings in their retelling of these events. If I were writing, I think I might have conveniently omitted some of these details.

Ah, but wouldn't that have been the way the Pharisees and Sadducees would have handled it? Write a story that doesn't reveal anything wrong or dumb about yourself. The yeast of the Pharisees and Sadducees included arrogance, self-righteous pride, judgmentalism, and cold-heartedness. The fact that this story includes the disciples' lack of understanding shows they managed to reach a point of letting go of self—of delighting in God's grace that's demonstrated through their honest remembering. As I read and see that they're not bigger than life, I take heart, knowing that if God can work through them, surely God can also work through me!

My best friend in seminary was (and continues to be) a person with wonderful charisma born out of talents blended with transparent foibles. While people admired him, it was his humanness, his ability to humorously bare his weaknesses, that helped us be close to him. I learned through him the freedom that comes from openly laughing at my own shortcomings, and the wisdom that knows the gift we give each other as we lower our guard. Whether in self-help groups or one-on-one, whenever someone shares their struggles, someone else feels safe to do the same. Such sharing is a powerful gift.

The disciples gave us the story of God's grace through telling about Jesus. They also lived the truth of this grace by being willing to depict themselves truthfully. Through their honesty, we are given the confidence that we, too, can be truthful and self-revealing. We can do this where we feel loved—in our homes and with our families, with our friends and in our churches. God's love frees us to be leaven of grace.

Where do you find it most easy to be truthful and honest about yourself?

Dear God, give me courage to be honest about myself, grace to be able to laugh at myself, and gratitude for those who love me as I am.

Wednesday: Daring to Let Go

Read Matthew 16:13-28. *"For those who want to save their life will lose it, and those who lose their life for my sake will find it"* (v. 25).

I WOKE IN THE MIDDLE OF THE NIGHT and struggled to get back to sleep. My thoughts began to spin, replaying themselves while my body wished they would stop. Anxiety increased with the thought that when morning comes I'll be short on sleep. With that thought, the insomnia seemed to grow in strength.

Fortunately, I had read this text before turning in. It gave me some diversion in my sleeplessness. I realized that I was experiencing what Jesus warned against and the opposite of what he was promoting. I was focused on myself and my own thoughts, and thus I was hurting myself. I tried to think of ways in which I've positively experienced the wisdom of losing myself.

When I was in seventh grade, an age more than any other when we are preoccupied with self, I had to give a two-minute talk about some current event. I was very nervous about speaking in front of the class in that formal way. When I began to talk, my kneecap began a nervous twitch. It happened that I was wearing a pair of very lightweight pants, so the twitch was amplified by the fabric of the trousers. They looked as if they were blowing in the wind. Of course, the front row was well entertained and made sure everyone else discovered the source of their amusement. The more the giggling increased, the more my knees knocked. The end of the talk couldn't come fast enough.

While some nervousness at speaking in front of people has never left me completely, I've grown in experience and self-confidence, making public speaking easier. More importantly, I have discovered that the more focused I am on what I want to say, the less I think about how I am doing. When this speaking is a sermon, it is a time when I lose myself in Jesus and my passion for telling his story. It is a wonderful feeling—to realize the communication is working because those listening are also passionate about the subject matter. The feeling is also wonderful because I experience the paradox that I'm doing well because I don't care how I'm doing. I'm caring more about the message than the messenger.

Jesus not only promised that to lose one's life can be lifegiving, he lived this teaching. It was connected to his knowledge that he had to go to Jerusalem. From this point on in Matthew he speaks plainly about his impending death and resurrection—though how much the disciples understood him is uncertain. As the years passed, however, and as they would be faced with putting themselves at risk in order to be public about their faith, their passion to follow Jesus would overwhelm notions of putting self first.

Most of us may not face life choices in which our physical well-being is put at risk as we follow paths of faith. Most life choices that put this teaching of Jesus to the test are much more constant and subtle. It is an endeavor that is made more difficult if I focus on how I must let go of myself. If I were to approach giving a public speech by focusing on the need to not think about myself, I would, in effect, be thinking about myself. It won't work that way. No, the focus needs to be on the subject matter and our passion for it. The subject matter of our daily life is Jesus. We are called not so much to a letting go of self, as we are called to a letting go into Jesus.

———◆◆◆◆———

List the ways that loving Jesus will play out for you today.

Lord Jesus, may my love for you shape everything I do and say this day.

Week Five ⟶

Thursday: A State of Grace

Read Matthew 17. *"This is my Son, the Beloved; with him I am well pleased; listen to him!"* (v. 5).

F OR THE SECOND TIME, the voice of God speaks. Words heard at Jesus' baptism are repeated—this time, with the addendum, "Listen to him!"

At this point in Jesus' ministry, these words seem fitting. Think of all the things Jesus has done—the healings, the miracles of feedings and walking on water, the teachings, and the passion for justice and compassion in the face of harsh criticism. No wonder God says, "With him I am well pleased."

The first time God spoke these words was more unusual. At the point of Jesus' baptism, we know very little about Jesus. In Matthew's telling of the story, Jesus hasn't done anything to warrant God's approval by the time he appears at the Jordan River. If I were God, I would have been more inclined to wait a little, see how he does, and then speak those words only after Jesus had a bit of experience under his belt and had proven himself worthy of praise. God is more generous than I am.

A few years ago I was present for a friend's fiftieth birthday party. It was a surprise her husband had orchestrated. A few dozen of us squeezed around her in their living room. She sat on the fireplace hearth opening a variety of gifts. In the middle of it she stopped, looked at all of us and said, "I just love this—that you're all here for me." We laughed with her joyful statement, and she continued. "What I mean is, a birthday party is my favorite celebration. It is the one time we gather around someone and celebrate them for no other reason than that they are. I haven't done anything, won any kind of an award, and yet here you are. This is the best. Thank you all for being here." Her words were full of grace and truth. Birthday parties are the best—rejoicing in someone just because they are.

In blessing Jesus at the outset of his ministry, God showed us that love is not conditional upon Jesus' performance. Grace is a given. "Behold, my son. He hasn't done a thing yet, but I am pleased with him, and I want everyone to know it."

Grace is not conditional. God gives us life, births us daily, and celebrates our being daily. We wake each day with God's blessing: "Behold. This is my creation, with whom I am pleased."

God's blessing was given a second time. In their shared vision experience, Peter, James, and John heard God's voice more pointedly directed to themselves. An executive order is given: "Listen to him."

Remember the exercise in reading Scripture with the Benedictine method? Stop your reading for a moment. It's like my wife saying, "Andrew, put the paper down and look into my eyes." This is important. The disciples—we—have heard the voice of God. It may be the only words we hear directly spoken by God: a command to listen to someone, not obey, or follow, or believe, or organize. Just listen. Listen deeply with an open mind and a responsive heart. God is confident the rest will follow.

Listening to Jesus is more than reading his words in the Gospels. It is finding a way to put the paper down, looking deeply into his heart, and hearing Christ speak to our soul. God is confident the rest will follow. We are, after all, God's children. We are made with the ability to hear, and made with hearts meant to love.

Which teachings of Jesus have been the most important for you?

Ever-present God, may I hear what you are telling me today? (Take a moment to be silent, to see what comes to mind. Trust that God speaks to you.)

Friday: The Greatest

Read Matthew 18:1-14. *"Truly I tell you, unless you change and become like children, you will never enter the kingdom of heaven. Whoever becomes humble like this child is the greatest in the kingdom of heaven"* (vv. 3-4).

His name was David. I think he must have been about six years old. I met him once on a walk in the small woods by our home. Our dogs met first. David was walking near his father, swinging a stick and enjoying the whipping sound of it cutting through the air. "Looks like you've got a good bodyguard there," I said to his dad. "The best!" was his instant response. David was deep into his world, oblivious to our enjoyment of his theatrics.

"What's your name?" I queried.

"David."

"Good name. My middle name is David."

He nodded, both in acknowledgment and, it seemed, by way of saying, "That's enough of adult talk. I have things to do." So his father and I engaged in small talk for the next hundred yards while David led the way.

As we reached the wash in the gully and the foot bridge that crossed it, David jumped forward with a loud "hunh!" Like some ninja or wrestler posed before combat, and with stick in hand, he might as well have yelled "en garde!"

I asked him, "What's up, David?"

"You have to be ready for the trolls when we cross this bridge!" he replied. The trolls seemed as real to him as the feelings of joy in his presence were real to me.

A walk in the woods—or anywhere—is far more interesting in the presence of a child. A child's mind is alive with imagination and possibility, while mine tends to be narrowed by past experience. I think I take it all in, but I walk by everything. A child picks up a plain rock and makes it worth saving because he claimed it. My sons would want to collect a great many things I wanted to leave behind. Even pieces of bark were worthy of a collection. Nothing was beyond their redemption.

The Apostle Paul wrote in his most famous chapter, "When I was a child, I spoke like a child, I thought like a child, I reasoned like a child; when I became an adult, I put an end to childish ways" (I Cor. 13:11). I know that Paul was encouraging Christian maturity, but his words strike me as sad ones in the midst of so many words of beauty. And I wonder if he never heard the story of Jesus honoring a child, teaching that unless we become like little children, we cannot enter the realm of heaven.

I cannot imagine that my young friend David would ponder very long the meaning of Jesus' words. But my adult mind wonders about all sorts of things in this text. Is heaven a place or a state of being? What would it mean to humble myself—be unassuming or discount myself or be completely honest in self-assessment? Did Jesus use an opposite meaning of "greatest" in responding to the disciples—greatness that comes from God and not from human acclaim? And becoming "like little children"—am I to assume that means things like being playful, quick to seek affection, trusting, imaginative, full of wonder? Does it include childhood fears and sassiness and temper tantrums?

My adult mind may not sort out all my questions. Perhaps Jesus doesn't want me to. It might be best if I would have a David with me while these words are read, or some other little one who squirms in the pews and makes too much noise for my adult sensibilities. One who, upon hearing Jesus' words, nods in acknowledgment that at some level she is heard and accepted. One who takes it for granted that she is cared for and loved. That is a gift. That is the greatest. We are, after all, simply and most importantly, God's children.

❖

What is your favorite Bible story from childhood? What made it your favorite?

Dear God, may I always see myself simply as your child, loved by you.

Saturday: When Forgiveness Doesn't Come

Read Matthew 18:15-35. *"The kingdom of heaven may be compared to a king who wished to settle accounts with his slaves"* (v. 23).

Forgiveness is complex. I'm not sure it's as simple as Jesus makes it sound when he says we must forgive "seventy-seven times" (Matt. 18:22). I can imagine forgiving my own child that many times if it's for something as minor and predictable as sassiness. Besides, I might have pushed him to it. But forgiveness for an extreme offense is another issue.

Called upon for counsel, I have listened to people who have spoken of their life as a victim of spouse or child abuse or incest. They sometimes have been told they must forgive, because Jesus said to. With indignation, they refuse, feeling that to do so is to be doubly abused. Refusing forgiveness feels like a step in regaining rights that were torn away.

I tend to support their instincts and their anger that refuses to forgive. Some sufferings are hideous and should not be bandaged so quickly. Even with healing, a scar will likely remain. Perhaps for God, forgiveness is like wiping the slate clean, but between humans, forgiveness is more like being willing to close a door on the past and finding ways to go on.

What do you tell a person, for example, whose spouse promises they won't drink again, who begs for forgiveness knowing that intoxication unleashed verbal and/or physical abuse? Must the injured person forgive? Jesus said, "seventy-seven times." The chaos of emotion is enormous: intense anger, grief for lost dreams and time, guilt for feelings of vengeance, shame for the mess of life and perhaps harm to children, despair, confusion, and bleak resignation. Should a person be forgiven in these circumstances? And if so, what does that mean?

When I give counsel to someone in a bind like this, I make a clear distinction between forgiveness and protection from further victimization. I encourage them to treat forgiveness as the second order of business. The first order is to take steps to assure that they will not continue to be victimized. The loving thing to do before forgiveness is to stop the sin from repeating. Jesus fought patterns and conditions that led people to sin. It is right that victims of sin be encouraged to do the same.

It is time to think about forgiveness when a person feels safe from further harm. Where the wound is deep, I am not in a rush to cover it over. Justified anger can be cathartic for a while if kept from becoming a blind lashing out, creating a new set of problems. It is a positive force when channeled into asserting one's rights, bolstering courage for difficult action, and raging at injustice. There comes a point, however, when the door needs to be closed on suffering from another's wrongdoing. If a person's life is consumed by this, then a victim is doubly victimized and their tomorrow is taken from them. If forgiveness does not come, perhaps release will.

In certain instances I have found that even when people want to forgive and let go, they may still find it impossible to will that to happen. I then encourage them to use a process of meditation: "Imagine that you are in the presence of God. Put your hands on the package that represents your hurt and your anger. You know you can't forgive, or heal, or let it go. But you give that package to God. Ask God to handle it for you and make it happen. Trust that God will help you."

Jesus describes the realm of heaven as one in which the ruler desires to settle accounts. God makes this so for us and will help make it so between us.

—•◦•◦•—

If there is an unresolved issue of hurt in your life, try the meditation process described earlier.

Thank you God, for always offering me forgiveness. Strengthen me for loving actions.

SUNDAY: ONE SHOE DOESN'T FIT ALL

Read Matthew 19:1-15. *"Is it lawful for a man to divorce his wife for any cause?"* (v. 3).

ONE OF THE GIFTS OF PARENTHOOD are moments when you can take a step back and consider who your children are—just to take them in and enjoy them.

Many parents of more than one child may marvel that their children can be so different. It is a kind of relief to know that who their children are is a great deal of their own doing. A parent can take a little credit or a little blame—but not much. Parenting means providing good soil, water, and sunshine for each seed to grow. The seeds are different, however, and each will respond differently. Love adjusts for each person and each circumstance. Sooner or later, it seems, every rule and every response is adjusted to fit the occasion.

So it was with Jesus. He treated different people and different situations differently. He told a wealthy young man to sell all his possessions, give to the poor, and come and follow.

84

To another wealthy man, Zacchaeus, he gave praise because Zacchaeus gave half his wealth away. With his good friend Lazarus, however, Jesus said nothing about his wealth and giving it away. Jesus treats each person and each situation differently. It is the way of love.

We cannot take every statement of Jesus and apply them to another situation and expect it to work. A couple in their fifties came to me many years ago seeking advice. One had been widowed for a few years. The other had divorced many years before, after a very difficult marriage. There had been no infidelity, however, and now they were haunted by Jesus' teaching that branded a remarriage to be adulterous. They weren't sure they could live with that. What was my counsel?

I couldn't help but admire their devotion to Jesus and his teachings. I wondered, "What would Jesus say if he were in my place, face to face with a sweet older couple who carried the heartache of loss or brokenness in their memory, but who now longed to build a loving future together?" I believe Jesus would have spoken words of blessing and encouragement to them, as I did.

Jesus spoke those very harsh words about divorce and remarriage because women were vulnerable to being treated callously, as property. A man could, with little—if any—reason, divorce a woman, leaving her in a very precarious situation. Shamed and shunned, with no recourse for justice or protection of property or means of support, how could a woman manage? Jesus' words reveal his compassion for those who might be abandoned and his anger for those who looked to justify their cruelty.

In our culture where there is so much brokenness, Jesus would be deeply concerned to protect the sanctity of marriage. And care must be taken not to explain away his teachings that may seem difficult. But as I think about this teaching on divorce, I also remember when Jesus encountered a Samaritan woman at a well. Then he simply stated she had been married five times and was not married to the man with whom she was living. No condemnation, just statement of fact. Love encountered this person in a different way. Love left her with a longing for life-giving water, and the joy of having found it.

Today's reading again shows Jesus "speaking the truth in love" (Eph. 4:15). What are the situations where you have the opportunity to do the same?

Thank you for loving me. As I read your words, may I learn how your love continues to teach, correct, and encourage me.

Monday: The Treasures God Gives

Read Matthew 19:16-30. *"Teacher, what good deed must I do to have eternal life?"... Jesus said to him, "If you wish to be perfect, go, sell your possessions, and give the money to the poor, and you will have treasure in heaven; then come, follow me"* (vv. 16, 21).

A NIECE INVITED ME TO OFFICIATE and preach at her wedding. The ceremony was in a gorgeous outdoor setting in northern Minnesota. Huge pines formed our cathedral's walls, with a deep blue sky as our vaulted ceiling. My opening words were fitting for the setting, but left people wondering if they were fitting for the occasion:

"On the shores of the nearby lake, guests of this lodge enjoy the thrill of bald eagles soaring overhead or perched in tall pines by the water's edge. It is a joy that's been preserved for us in no small measure because of the prophetic voice of Rachel Carson. Forty some years ago her book, *Silent Spring*, warned us of the deadly implications of the chemical DDT. Bald eagles and many other species were at grave risk because this chemical made their egg shells too fragile, causing sharply reduced birth rates. The thought of a silent spring, of the loss of the choir of bird songs that surround us now, electrified our country to take action and protect the abundant beauty that is so precious to us.

"The wisdom of God can be seen in this truth: What is most precious for our life, God gives in the greatest abundance. The beautiful blue of the sky above us also means clean air to breathe and a shield from harmful radiation. The water nearby is also the reason there is life on this earth. The love between people that is so abundant in this occasion is more important than any possession we have brought with us to this day. These are the things God gives in the greatest abundance—that which is most precious for life.

"This is a time to reaffirm the wisdom of God. Now we state clearly that the song of the birds, the air we breathe, the water we drink, and the love that undergirds your marriage— these are the things that are most precious to us. These are what give us life and joy. These are what we will promote and preserve. We will not take them for granted nor wait for their endangerment before we treasure them.

"It is with a sense of irony, therefore, that the bonds of your love will be symbolized by golden rings. What God has made the least of in this world is also the least important for our lives. Your rings will only be precious to you if you grow in what you have in greatest abundance—your love for each other."

Jesus was also asked to speak words of guidance by one who was looking to do the right thing. Though not in the context of a wedding, the rich young ruler is wanting to do what is right for a good life, and Jesus' response is based in the same wisdom of God at the heart of my wedding sermon.

The threat of a silent spring or the abundance of love at a wedding are not the only ways we learn what is precious in God's reckoning. When American college students return from study in developing countries, especially if they were living with an average citizen of the host country, they are amazed and moved by the happiness and generosity of those who have so little. Good friends just returned from helping with the World Health Organization, inoculating children in a community that bordered the Sahara Desert. The community had not had rain in four years, yet the first thing my friends were offered upon their arrival was what was most precious to the villagers—a glass of clear water. (At the same time, a young girl was preparing her camel for the fourteen- mile round trip to the nearest well for her family's water.) In gratitude for my friends' precious gift of abundant health for their children, the villagers were wanting to sacrifice their one goat for a thanksgiving meal in their honor.

Wealth and power and a drive for perfection seemed to dominate the life of the rich young ruler. I believe Jesus' words were spoken in love, spoken to one whose heart and treasure were absorbed by the least abundant and least precious of God's gifts.

Life that God gives, clean air and water, the love of family and friends, creative minds and hands, the ability to give of ourselves for the good of God's creation, the hope of eternal life, the presence of God's spirit, these God gives in abundance. These are what we treasure as we respond to Jesus' invitation, "Follow me."

———◆◆◆◆———

Write down at least ten things in your life that you value the most. How do these ten compare with the wisdom of God's abundance as described above?

Dear God, help me to nurture and protect what you give in abundance. Help me not take for granted that which you give in plenty.

TUESDAY: IT'S YOUR CALL

Read Matthew 20:1-16. *"When those hired about five o'clock came, each of them received the usual daily wage. Now when the first came, they thought they would receive more; but each of them also received the usual daily wage. And when they received it, they grumbled against the landowner"* (vv. 9-11).

JESUS' STORY OF THE WORKERS all receiving the same pay—no matter when they were hired—is recorded only by Matthew. Those hired first probably represent the Israelites who responded to God's call, beginning with the Covenant with Abraham and Sarah. We assume this story anticipates new Gentile converts and their equal partnership in God's family. And we can also imagine that people who had been in it from the ground floor were unsure about Johnny-come-latelys reaping the same rewards as they.

I suppose if a job were difficult and unpleasant, I would grumble, too, if I were paid the same as someone who did half the work. There's hardly an office today where the hard-working core of a business doesn't have doubts about the worth of many in upper-level management.

This is not a story about a line job in a factory, however. This is about being a part of God's road crew. I once told some children this story, but I changed the setting from a field to a birthday party. Some kids were there for the whole event, while others came late and missed almost the whole party. When the party was over, they were all given the same bag of party gifts. Was that fair? The children who heard the tale about the party understood Jesus' story. Not only did they think it was fair that the latecomers got the same party gifts, they felt so bad for those who missed most of the party that they wondered if the latecomers shouldn't have been given more than those who had the fun of the whole party!

I had a similar conversation with some middle-aged dog-walking acquaintances. After describing some of the things my son was doing and the passion he was feeling for doing them, a couple of them responded, "Gee, I wish I felt some passion for anything. I'm still trying to figure out what I'm doing with my life!" They were serious. They were longing to be called into a field of labor where they could offer themselves in life-giving ways.

One of the reasons we love Jesus' stories is because, like all good stories, they are timeless and universal. They have a way of drawing us in and inviting us to find their meaning for our lives. In this story, the field of labor is a vineyard. But we know it's an allegory and that the vineyard is anywhere we find ourselves. We also know that it is God who calls us; the lucky ones know this from the get-go.

I don't think it matters terribly to God what our labor in the vineyard is. My mother's passion and gift was making everyone—from the butcher to the visiting dignitary—feel important and valued. My mechanic's gift was bailing people out of their car woes on a daily basis. My infirm uncle in a nursing home daily carried hundreds of people in prayer. And so the stories go in God's vineyard, where the workers feel profoundly blessed to be able to give themselves, each in their own way.

Who do you know who are models of workers in God's vineyard? What makes them so?

Gracious God, may I plunge into the life that's been given me, trusting the privilege of working in your vineyard.

Wednesday: Counter Culture

Read Matthew 20:17-34. *"You know that the rulers of the Gentiles lord it over them, and their great ones are tyrants over them. It will not be so among you; but whoever wishes to be great among you must be your slave . . ."* (vv. 25-26).

At the conclusion of my seminary education, I spent a year in some additional training. Part of that year I worked for the majority caucus in our state legislature. The work intensified as newly elected legislators were sworn in, as everyone received committee assignments, and as office space was divided up.

My fellow researchers clued me in to a phenomenon I might have otherwise ignored the intensity of feeling and competition for certain office spaces. Two factors seemed most important: square footage and proximity to the people with power. Those with the most power had corner offices with the most square footage. First-year legislators of the minority party were likely to be assigned the smallest, most poorly placed spaces. When I naively expressed surprise at this revelation, I was told that aides or legislators themselves might sometimes take a measuring tape into different offices to verify the exact square footage.

I was a bit disillusioned with this knowledge, but it seems Jesus knew long ago that people have all sorts of ways to show their importance and power.

Just as stubbornness or pride are not limited to any one culture or clan, lording power over others was not unique to the Gentiles. From being a playground bully or a devious wheeler-dealer, to being sharp witted or sharper tongued, humans exercise power in a variety of ways. We are able to reflect on these patterns. Moreover, we are capable of deciding how to channel our instincts for power. Jesus calls us to a higher way.

It is said that Gautama Buddha, as he fasted beneath a bo tree, received his great revelations as his body was near death. He knew that he could choose to enter heaven (nirvana) at that point, but he also longed to bring his insights into the world for the benefit of humanity. Rather than die, he chose to live. His teachings have served countless generations who had been living with a hopeless cycle of life and death. The Buddha saw his life work to be one of service.

What is the purpose of our life on this earth? Can it be summarized by the old Bavarian proverb, "Work. Work. Save. Save. Buy a house. Croak"? Is there more to what God hopes for us than believing in Jesus so that we can live in the next life? Or does Jesus call us to service in this life?

Jesus does not ask us to reject power, but to decide how to use power. The purpose of our life is to use our power, our skills, and our wits in service to one another and this amazing creation. When God, in Genesis, gave humans the gift of "dominion" over creation, this is the exact opposite of "domination." God calls us to be of service—that is the highest calling and the greatest path.

Think of how easy it would have been for Jesus to use his power to be the greatest, the top of the pecking order. Instead, he turned down the tempter's enticement to do just that. He chose a path of obedience and service out of love for God and God's creation. Jesus believes we are also capable of this path of love.

⬦⬦⬦⬦

When have you decided to channel your power for service?

Creating God, who has given me the power to affect others for good or ill, may I choose paths of love and service.

Week Six ➜

Thursday: Gathering Storm Clouds

Read Matthew 21. *When the chief priests and the Pharisees heard his parables, they realized that he was speaking about them. They wanted to arrest him, but they feared the crowds, because they regarded him as a prophet* (vv. 45-46).

The days in the life of Jesus were mostly sunny. There were days of beautiful teachings on the mount, healings, exorcisms, and assorted miracles—days upon days of praise and followers and throngs hurrying to be blessed by his presence. There were visions and adventures and stories to last a lifetime. Once in a while the sunshine was interrupted by rumblings and the occasional thundering of religious authorities trying to rain on the parade. Finally, in his last days, two major weather systems came together in Jerusalem. In their clash, huge thunderclouds arose, and boiling winds focused into a hurricane of controversy and confrontations. But for Jesus, there was no turning back.

In his entry into Jerusalem there is a sense of almost reckless abandon. Jesus was committed to speaking the truth and confronting the entrenched patterns that were contrary to the love of God. Vendors and money-changers were scattered because they were gouging pilgrims from around the world. The religious establishment was scolded for being unresponsive to the signs and teachings of God's presence.

Even a hapless, unproductive fig tree withered in the onslaught of Jesus' whirlwind. Jesus never seemed to be guided by fear and avoidance, but was driven by love and the hope of redemption.

When I was first being trained in counseling, I was apprenticed to a child and family therapist. I participated in frequent sessions in which a teen or parent was asked these questions: "What are you afraid of? What is the worst that can happen? If the worst happens, what then?" The therapist knew that people often get stuck in a situation because they are afraid of something, but may not face their fear. If people can name their fears, it helps them move beyond patterns of avoidance. In confronting a situation, we have more strength to deal with things if we have decided in advance that we'll be okay—even if the worst happens.

Jesus told his disciples, "We're going to Jerusalem. I'm going to be betrayed, and I'm going to die. That's the worst that's going to happen. But even the worst will not hold me back. I will be raised to life." Because Jesus faced the fears and the worst-case scenarios, he was free for action—the action we see unleashed in this chapter of Matthew's Gospel.

All of us know what it is like to live in fear and avoidance. We may choose to ignore problems in the hope that they will resolve themselves and go away. There is a price. It takes tremendous energy to sit with our fears, to lose sleep, to repress our feelings, to stew and fret. Finally something happens to break down the dam holding all this back. While it can be messy, there is also a sense of released energy—knowing that the chain of events is at last unfolding.

Jesus shows us the way through deadly situations into life. For a time he steered clear of Jerusalem. But going there was in the back of his mind. Prayer was a constant companion, strengthening his resolve to face his fears and enter the fray. At last, the game was at hand.

There was little reason to be tentative or cautious. He practiced what he preached: "those who lose their life will find it" (Matt. 10:39). The storm raged, swift currents swept him along, and Jesus never seemed more alive.

———◆◆◆◆———

What fears and difficulties have you avoided? What helped you face them? What help did faith provide?

God who is always with me, may I name my fears and deal with them, trusting that you will help see me through.

FRIDAY: LOVE DOES NOT INSIST

Read Matthew 22. *"You are wrong, because you know neither the scriptures nor the power of God. 'Teacher, which commandment in the law is the greatest?' He said to him, 'You shall love the Lord your God with all your heart, and with all your soul, and with all your mind. This is the greatest and first commandment. And a second is like it; You shall love your neighbor as yourself. On these two commandments hang all the law and the prophets'"* (vv. 29, 36-40).

IN A CONVERSATION TODAY with a newly met neighbor, one thing led to another. While our dogs frolicked in the woods, he spoke of his concerns about politics, about the blurring of healthy lines between church and state, and about his sister's literal interpretation of the Bible. Her rigid, closed mindedness was difficult for him to bear. I can imagine that she is also troubled by her brother's openness to truths he has found in the Ojibway or Buddhist traditions. I'm sure she prays that her brother finds his way to the truth, accepting Jesus in the same way she does.

Jesus engaged in debate with people who are as passionate as we are. Some of our issues are similar to theirs: Is capital punishment allowed? Is there a resurrection—and, if so, which spouse will you join in heaven? How can there be a good, all-powerful God if terrible things happen? And some of our questions were unknown to them: Should our children be taught evolution? Shall same-sex couples be allowed to marry? Should human fetal tissue be used for genetic engineering?

Jesus handled questions differently. With some, like the seven spouses in heaven dilemma, he gave a direct answer. With other questions, he avoided simple answers while nudging the adversary into deeper thoughts—like the question about paying taxes. Then there were the challenges to the motivation behind the question, knowing the question was not the issue.

Matthew places the question of the greatest commandment as the last to be answered by Jesus. It is as though to say, "In the end, all the teachings, all the responses to God and to one another, all the different ways of answering questions and understanding God, all of them are secondary to this simple word: love." We are to love God, love neighbor, love self. Chances are, if we poured as much energy into loving as we do into debating our notions of truth and insisting on our own ways, the points of disagreement would fade into points for amusement.

My encounter today in the woods with a new neighbor reminded me of a discussion I had at a Boy Scout camp with another assistant scoutmaster. When he saw a book I was carrying and learned I had training at a camp called "The Tracker," he told me that he once was fascinated by that body of learning until he became a Christian. I prodded him about why that changed his interest. "Well, they don't teach that Jesus is the only path to a relationship with God and to heaven." A lengthy discussion followed, which I'm sure left him praying for my misunderstandings and my everlasting soul. I think he was horrified that I so much believe in a God of love, that I think it likely that somehow nothing in heaven or earth can ever truly separate any soul from God's deep, deep love.

We all have questions. We may never find full agreement in our answers. Jesus had remarkable ways of handling the wide array of questions posed to him. Shaping each response was the spirit of love. We are guided by this. As important as we may make the content of our answers, we know that it is more important to be loving of one another while we seek clear answers.

◆•◆•◆

How does love "not insist on its own way" when there are religious disagreements?

Loving God, as I seek answers to questions, help me speak with others in loving, honest, and gentle ways.

Saturday: Past and Present

Read Matthew 23. *"Woe to you . . . Jerusalem, Jerusalem, the city that kills the prophets and stones those who are sent to it! How often have I desired to gather your children together as a hen gathers her brood under her wings, and you were not willing"* (v. 37).

A CENTURY AGO PHILOSOPHER GEORGE SANTAYANA taught that those who do not remember their past, are condemned to repeat it. The Christian tradition faithfully returns to its origins, not in refusal to face the present day, but to live this day well, having learned the lessons of our past. We know that while the structures of humanity may be quite different from two thousand years ago, humans themselves are much the same. Therefore, our study and reflection, our journey with Matthew through Lent, is the knowledge that through this story of the past, we hold a mirror before us and see ourselves.

There are two impressions I see in the mirror of Matthew's twenty-third chapter. The first has to do with what I think Jesus was feeling in this lengthy tirade against the teachers of the law and the Pharisees. There seems to be something deeper than his anger. The crowds and his disciples are present. We assume the teachers of the law and the Pharisees are among them, or listening from the fringe. After several issues are spelled out clearly, Jesus concludes with a poignant lament. You can almost hear the tears of grief in his words, "How I longed to gather you, but you would not." It is grief borne out of his love for them that causes him to be so angry.

Many years ago a friend described grief to me as "the process of letting go of unfulfilled dreams." Jesus knew he had no more than a few days left. He knew the religious establishment was not responding to him or his message. He knew they were more interested in preserving tradition than giving way to truth. He knew that his dream of transforming them by and for love, would not come to pass. At this moment of letting go of a dream his heart was heavy. We see his grief in his anger. Anger is often the first stage of grief. Is this not a mirror that can help us in our life?

The second impression of history breaking into present reality is what happens when I hear the grief in Jesus' voice. As I read the last three verses of this chapter slowly, I can hear how his heart is breaking. If I hear only someone's anger, I am likely to remain detached, or maybe defensive and belligerent. But if I hear another's pain, my heart softens, and there is a chance I will drop my defenses. Jesus directs his anger at those he grieves for. He grieves and is angry, not because he hates them, but because he loves them deeply.

I feel Jesus' grief. Yet I cannot shake some sadness that knows I can be like the teachers of the law and the Pharisees. I do not always practice what I preach. I am sometimes motivated by wanting others to notice and praise me. I can lose perspective and get wrapped up in petty issues while neglecting "justice, mercy, and faithfulness."

I need not repeat their past, however. I see their past, but I do not choose to repeat their story. I have no reason to pretend I am perfect. There is no joy in keeping God at arm's length. Jesus calls out in love. Into the arms of Jesus I fly.

What lost dreams have caused you grief? When have your defenses lowered?

Wide open are your arms, O God, and I, your child, fall into your love, amazed to be the object of your longing.

Sunday: The Heart of Our Home

Read Matthew 24. *"Heaven and earth will pass away, but my words will not pass away"* (v. 35).

An unexpected thing happened to me with my mother's death. In her eighties, and after a few years of enduring cancer, her last days came gently. We were fortunate that a granddaughter could be her housemate during the last year in her home of forty-five years. The family also had the support of Hospice.

As her body was dying, most of the immediate family was near. With the few hours that would be private, before the morticians came for her, alone and together we had moments for prayer and tears and goodbyes and singing, "Lord, now lettest thou thy servant depart in peace, according to thy word. For mine eyes have seen thy salvation, which thou has prepared before the face of all people."

The morticians were kind and discreet. We left them to their familiar tasks. I think most of us were frozen in a surreal parade. Our minds knew our mother, our grandmother (or at least her body), was contained in the corduroy bag wheeled out on the gurney. How could it be that we would never see the flash of her smile or the sparkle in those brown eyes again? We escorted her to the van, mutely standing by on the front lawn. Who could have prepared us with any rite of passage for that moment? Some events unfold in their own way, leaving us to look back upon their tracks in our memory to find the path that was made.

As the van pulled away and I turned to go back into the house, the unexpected dawned on me. This great old house we simply called 1555, that had welcomed me when I was six, was now empty for me. The heart and soul of it had just left. What did this house mean anymore? Without Mother's voice calling to every footfall that crossed the threshold, "Who's that comin' in my door?" there was nothing that could really hold me to this piece of real estate. I could give it up.

Matthew's twenty-fourth chapter almost overwhelms us with Jesus' many warnings of the end times. It begins as he is walking by this amazing new temple built by Herod. It would be huge even by today's standards—more than three football fields in length. Whether Matthew knew of its destruction by the Romans in A.D. 70 as he wrote his gospel, we wonder. This we do know: Jesus calls us to remember that which endures and that which does not. The earth will pass away. Even heaven, Jesus says, will pass away. But his words will not. It is the words of Jesus that become the heart and soul of all that is. Without them, life is empty.

Perhaps this prophecy seared itself into the mind and heart of John as he set the foundation for his Gospel with that same brilliant truth: "In the beginning was the Word, and the Word was with God, and the Word was God . . . All things came into being through him, and without him not one thing came into being. What has come into being in him was life, and the life was the light of all people" (John 1:1-4).

What makes this earth a treasure and a home worth protecting? It is the presence of the Word, the Christ, that makes it possible for there to be the blue of the sky, the green of leaves, the cool mists and driving rains, the song of the chickadee rising above blizzard winds. What makes my life worth living fully? It is the presence of Christ, whose word fills me with life and forever holds my soul. What gives our tomorrows the promise of dawn? It is knowing that even if all the signs and portents and heavy loads point to death, knowing that our home is always to be found in Christ, the heart and soul of our life.

Picture your home, your school, your workplace. Picture Jesus in each place. Does this change how you feel about and live in each place?

"When other helpers fail and comforts flee, Help of the helpless, Oh abide with me" (LBW #272).

Monday in Holy Week: A Compass, a Map, and a Paddle

Read Matthew 25. *"Keep awake therefore, for you know neither the day nor the hour"* (v. 13).

Many years ago, my lifelong friend, Morris Wee, and I arrived at Wilderness Canoe Base in northern Minnesota a day late. Mo's father drove us up the Gunflint Trail, reminiscing the whole way about his summer working on a logging crew in the 1920s. The group we were joining for a month-long venture was already at a base camp about six miles away.

The camp's director, H. A. Muus (always called "Ham" because of his initials) didn't waste any time with us. His orientation was simple: "Can you swim? Can you paddle a canoe? Here's a map. Here's where your group is camping. Here's a compass, if you need it. Throw your dufflebags in the canoe and off you go." There was a twinkle in his eye, a knowing trust in us and the educational philosophy of "learning by doing." (Camps are, for good reason, more cautious now than they were thirty-seven years ago.)

Once we cleared the Palisades on Seagull Lake, the rollers from the westerly wind were breaking over the gunwales. An hour later, and on the shoreline at last, we found the campsite.

A compass, a map, and a paddle were what Jesus was giving his disciples. Not literally, of course. These navigational tools came in a most surprising way: in stories. I'm far more practical, and far less trusting. I'm sure I would leave a long list, just as I did in leaving my last parish where I served as an interim pastor. My lengthy memo to my successor began, "I'm sure you'll figure most of this out, but here are some things to help you out . . ." That wasn't Jesus' style.

Three stories, the last ones Jesus tells in Matthew's Gospel, are the guides he leaves them. The first story points to the need to be ready for the bridegroom, Jesus. Being vigilant like those in the wedding party means that my own comfort in this life may not be the first thing I take care of. The resources I have at my disposal are to be used for the purpose of the wedding, for the presence of Christ.

Our map is found in the second story, the one about the talents. God creates each one of us with a variety of skills, gifts, aptitudes, and passions. Use them. Use them to God's glory. You need not even know to what end you are using them. The important thing is to use them, trusting that they are God-given, and if used, will yield dividends. If your gift is sewing or singing, organizing or phone calling, speaking, listening, or praying, supporting or leading, dive in with your gift in any way you can. God's gifts provide the map of our life. Using the gifts moves us beyond what we can see and reveals the next adventure.

The third story, about the final judgment, invites us to think about where we, as followers of Jesus, give of ourselves, where we put our paddle in and pull. Jesus unfailingly lived with deep love for those who were hurting: the sick and downtrodden, the outcasts and those undervalued, the "least" in the world. Look around you. Most of us can think of who those may be. They are not alone. Our Lord is in them; invisible to most, but visible to the eyes of faith.

The church is a beacon of hope to those who walk in darkness, and they come knocking on our door. Just today, three calls came. A woman who struggles with mental illness, who our church has known for years, reached out for our help for a hearing of her case next week. (The bridegroom is coming.) Another called with concerns of illness and hospitalization. (I can go there. I have gifts for that and must not keep them buried.) A foreign student called needing help with medical bills. (Ah, thanks to a "discretionary fund" from members, the "least" need not turned away empty handed.)

Who shows confidence and trust in you? What does it mean that Jesus trusts you?

I am humbled, O God, that you trust me to care for this world you love. May I trust your presence for strength, as I follow you this day.

TUESDAY IN HOLY WEEK: THE LONESOME VALLEY

Read Matthew 26:1-56. *And going a little farther, he threw himself on the ground and prayed, "My Father, if it is possible, let this cup pass from me; yet not what I want but what you want"* (v. 39).

AS A YOUNGSTER, I neither understood nor agreed with that great spiritual, "Jesus walked this lonesome valley. He had to walk it by himself. Oh, nobody else could walk it for him. He had to walk it by himself." Weren't his friends with him most of the way? And at the last, when they deserted him, wasn't God still with him? He wasn't really alone. My adolescent mind was right, in a sense.

With age and life experience, however, I understand this song better. There are times when a person not only feels alone, but is alone. There are times when God is silent.

You can just feel the forces pressing in upon Jesus and him pulling into himself. His energy that goes out for the good of others was spent with one last flourish, telling wonderful stories. Now Jesus turned and focused inward. "You know that after two days the Passover is coming, and the Son of Man will be handed over to be crucified." It's like being aware of someone at a party or a family gathering who seems to pull away into their own thoughts. Their body is there, but with a distant look in their eyes, you know their thoughts are somewhere else.

Matthew hints at this. While perfume was extravagantly poured on Jesus' head, Matthew notes that Jesus was aware of the disciples' complaint. He came out of his shell, and his rebuke reflects what's been on his mind: his death and burial. How heavy that burden must have been! Sometimes, when we carry heavy thoughts, being with people can heighten the

107

sense that the burdens we carry are ours alone. And it is lonely in the midst of others.

Jesus was with his disciples, but he knew he stood alone. He names their abandonment of him—Judas by betrayal and the others by desertion. Even if a few of them would have stayed at his side all the way to the cross, the next hours were still his to carry alone. As he broke the bread and poured out the wine, it was with the sense of "Take this. Take me. With this last gesture, I empty myself for you. I have nothing left to give."

Even though we walk a lonesome valley alone, we know the wisdom of alerting others to our ordeal. We seek their advice and comfort, knowing their thoughts, hearts, and prayers are with us on our walk. So Jesus also brings his friends to the garden where he will pray. He asks three to come with him further. The small comfort that might have come, if even one of them had managed to stand watch, was lost in their sleep. Only one would hear the fullness of his heart. Only God would know the depth of his sorrow, and the dread of what must come.

God listened. Listened full of love. Listened with a breaking heart. To pull Jesus off his chosen path would destroy the integrity of his life. Three times Jesus asked. Three times God heard but remained silent. Jesus' heart was heavy, knowing he had to walk the lonesome valley alone.

There is another who must have been near during those last days. Another who remained silent, but who, we know, had a breaking heart: Mary, Jesus' mother, who for a long time could only stand by and watch his days unfold. Mary represents every parent who knows the depth of tears that come when we see our children suffer. Every parent knows the

limits of their love; knows the longing to take our children—
no matter what their age—and protect them from all harm.

We see ourselves in Jesus and Mary. We know what it is
like to walk a lonesome valley alone. We know the sorrow of
not being able to rescue one we love from an ordeal. And we
know God's heart breaks, never sleeping when we walk alone.

———◆◆◆———

What have been your lonesome valleys? Who did you reach
out to? How did this person help?

*When I am alone, O God, may I remember that you hear my cry, and you
ever watch over me.*

WEDNESDAY IN HOLY WEEK: JUDAS REDEEMED

Read Matthew 26:57—27:26. *Pilate . . . took some water and washed
his hands before the crowd, saying, "I am innocent of this man's blood; see to it
yourselves"* (v. 27:24).

"OUT, DAMNED SPOT!" fumed Lady Macbeth as she tried to
remove the blood only she could see on her hands. In
Shakespeare's tragedy *Macbeth,* we listen in on the tortured
conscience of Lady Macbeth, who cannot erase the haunting
that dogs her thoughts for her role in the murder of King
Duncan. Try as she might, her guilty conscience will not let
her rest.

From the moment of Jesus' arrest through the time of
his conviction, all those responsible for his death are looking for some excuse, some way to wash their hands of the
role they'll play. The priests looked for a reason, even phony

charges, to justify their demand for Jesus' death. High Priest Caiaphas was relieved that Jesus gave them what was needed when he agreed that he was the Messiah. Tearing his robes, looking wounded, blaming Jesus with heresy—all sweeping actions that would not wash the blood from the hands of Caiaphas.

Silence in the face of injustice was Peter's choice. Avoiding any complicity, fearful for his own neck, Peter denied any association with Jesus. He washed his hands by disassociation. How often we avoid hard situations by steering clear or, as in Peter's case, by flat-out lying.

Pilate literally washed his hands of the whole matter. His rationalization was three-fold. First, in his mind, the good of the whole outweighed the wrong to the one. By sacrificing one, he thought to avoid a bigger problem. Secondly, he felt the pressure of the crowd and yielded to their lobby. Finally, he lamely attempted to see this as somebody else's issue. Jesus was not a Roman citizen, and therefore it wasn't Pilate's problem. Out came the water basin. Before all the world, he washed his hands. But his memory would not so easily wash the blood from them.

The irony of this section of Matthew's Gospel is that the one person who acted with dignity, who stepped forward and accepted responsibility for what was happening, was Judas. If there is such a thing as being worthy of redemption, Judas was the only one of the four so worthy. If only there had been some way for him to make his way to Jesus, to pour out his remorse at the throne of grace and be forgiven.

It must have been tempting for the followers who deserted Jesus to vilify Judas. Make him a scapegoat. Blame him for the chain of events that followed. Wash their hands by pointing to him as a villain. I suspect, however, that because so little other mention is made of him, they knew that he had been right to step forward and be accountable.

Each one of us has, at times, taken the part of Caiaphas, of Peter, and of Pilate, by acting with self-righteousness, lying, or avoidance. The surprise in today's reading is to discover that it is this moment in Judas' story that can guide us. Taking ownership for our sins, confessing before God, we can hope for our guilt to be removed and for healing to happen.

———————————

When have you experienced healing as a result of taking responsibility for wrongful actions?

God of grace, your love makes it possible for me to be honest when I fail you. May my honesty come quickly and may I accept your restoration wholly.

Week Seven ⟿

Thursday in Holy Week: Choosing to Die

Read Matthew 27:27-50. *Then Jesus cried again with a loud voice and breathed his last* (v. 50).

YESTERDAY I LISTENED TO A WOMAN SPEAK TENDERLY about her seventy-year-old brother whose death was imminent. Years ago he had chosen not to have prostate surgery. Now his days were coming swiftly to an end. He told his sister, "I'm ready to go. I'm at peace and want to go to heaven." She shared with pride, "He's leaving his family a lot of money from his small business. They'll be well taken care of. Not bad for a poor black boy from a family of eleven."

An hour later I heard a different story. I was on the phone listening to a woman whose brother-in-law has been given no more than six months to live. "He's not talking," she said. "He's in denial." I gave her some clues, some ways to approach the issue without making it sound as if she'd given up hope.

Running from death gives it more power than it should have. Facing death, coming to terms with it at some level, actually leaves us more able to embrace it and fight for life.

Jesus did not want to die. His prayers in the garden made that amply clear. Like all of us, he had a God-given love of life. At the same time, because he was able to speak of his own death, Jesus was strengthened to follow a path of truth-speaking and love-giving, which put him at risk. Jesus did not want to die. He chose to die, and it became his path to life. Because he lived with the reality of his heavenly home deep in his heart, he was strengthened to press on to the end. In doing so, he becomes a strength to us who are still on this side of life.

I also find strength in the patterns God shows us in our world. We watch the cycles of life and death and rebirth in all creation. Just as God has made it necessary for a caterpillar to end one form of existence in order to be transformed to the next, we know that the same is in store for us.

I cannot remember life in my mother's womb. I'm sure it must have been secure and comfortable. I imagine leaving her was painful, but I have forgotten. And I'm sure entry to heaven will be much the same.

Why God has chosen to give us life on this earth with death and resurrection as our birth into heaven, I do not know. It is the way that is given. I do not believe that God wants us to die tragically or before we've lived this stage of life fully. I do not think God decides, at a given moment, that anyone's "time is up, and they're needed in heaven."

I do not want to die. I have deeds to do, dreams to realize, flowers to smell, children to read to, and walks with no place to go.

I am not troubled by Jesus' last words in Matthew's account when Jesus spoke of being forsaken by God. Even these words are a sign of his faith, because they are the first line of Psalm 22—a shorthand way of preaching the whole psalm to those within earshot. It is a last gift for us all.

Some translations read, "He gave up his spirit." It was not taken from him. It was how Jesus lived his whole life: giving his spirit. My Lord and my God.

———•◦•◦•———

Take a moment, now or later, to read Psalm 22 and reflect on the impact on people who stood below the cross, who would begin to remember parts of this Psalm, and meditate on this while witnessing Jesus' death.

Lord Jesus, you show me how to live, and you show me how to die. Living and dying, my trust is in you.

Friday in Holy Week: A Quiet Strength

Read Matthew 27:51-66. *Many women were also there, looking on from a distance; they had followed Jesus from Galilee and had provided for him . . . So Joseph took the body and wrapped it in a clean linen cloth and laid it in his own new tomb, which he had hewn in the rock . . . Mary Magdalene and the other Mary were there, sitting opposite the tomb* (vv. 55, 59-61).

A first-year seminarian sat across the table from me. I asked her about her summer plans. She had just heard that she'd be in a summer CPE program—Clinical Pastoral Education—in a nearby hospital. She was both excited with the prospect and frightened by some stories that surround these programs because of their stress level and interpersonal intensity. I gave her my advice in a nutshell: "Remember, every study of patients in hospitals reveal that the most helpful person in their hospital stay is someone from housekeeping. The level of help is typically in inverse proportion to the person's place in the hierarchy of the hospital. Why are housekeeping people the most helpful?" I asked, not waiting for her to answer.

"Because they're down to earth, not intimidating to anyone, and they take time to listen while they putz around the room. Remember to learn from them."

Many who would become founders of the Christian church followed Jesus from Galilee to Jerusalem. After Jesus' death, women stepped forward, still caring for him. Joseph of Arimathea arranged for a proper burial. Quietly these people slip into the story to do what is needed. To the end, their tasks are simple, but Matthew knew their importance and honored them. Matthew gives the barest of details. It is like reading a page in the obituary: burial at such and such cemetery, with a light supper following at the church. The army of the faithful are there. They are the ones found busy in the kitchen, sewing countless quilts to give to the destitute, those who dish out food at shelters, those who regularly call someone who lives alone, those who see a need and step forward without being asked.

At my father's committal, our family and a few friends gathered by the graveside for a brief ceremony. I noticed the plot was dug in such a way that my mother wouldn't be buried between my father and brother, when her time came. Before leaving, I mentioned this to mom, and she was grateful for the chance to fix things the way she wanted, as I knew she would. This is where those who have come to care for our needs take over. The steward of the cemetery and the one at a discreet distance with the backhoe digger made the necessary arrangements. While the mourners were fed in the country church, cared for by more of God's quiet laborers, the two at the graves made things right. We returned just past sunset. A flock of white pelicans flew close by, and one trailed behind, the expectations are so big that it feels as if any words that might be spoken are dwarfed by comparison. What more can be said? The sparseness of each Gospel's treatment of Jesus' resurrection is quite remarkable, considering all the hoopla we've made of it since. But there it is; a whole ten verses that speak for themselves.

Why has Easter expanded so far beyond its rather simple original account? I wonder if the answer might be connected to other questions: Why did God choose to resurrect Jesus in this manner? Why not simply receive him into heaven as we assume Moses was, for example, because Moses appeared with Jesus in the transfiguration? Jesus has already spoken, at several points, of heaven and those who are already there. He has made it clear that God desires mercy—not sacrifice—so that's not what this is about. He has made it clear that God's power has always had the upper hand with the forces of evil. God could have let Jesus' story end with his death, and Jesus' life's work would have been complete. Then many would have been left wondering. And that's the point.

God chose to resurrect Jesus knowing our human need for it. Without it, doubts would flourish. God knew that we are like the Pharisees who always asked for one more sign from Jesus to prove himself. Knowing this, God raised Jesus from the dead. It's as if he said, "See, what he was telling you is true. He is the Messiah; the one I promised long ago; the fulfillment of ancient prophecies. See, what he told you is true. Nothing can separate you from my love. I do not lurk at a distance, ready to pounce on you when you fail. Instead, I walk with you, giving as much as I dare without taking over, so your life might be abundant. Look at him and know that everything he said is true. You have enough to go on now."

Even with the resurrection, many of us have periods in our lives when we wonder. I get nervous with over-exuberant Easter celebrations, because I know I have ways of shouting to hide what I don't know. The Easter story has been more of a quiet presence in my faith.

Long ago, when I would wander in the night and ask the big questions under the Milky Way, I could not make my way to belief. Logically, there seemed to be no answer to the ancient questions: How can eternity or space go infinitely? Where did God come from? Why do awful things happen? These are the questions that do not have an adequate answer. So rather than build a case on negation, on what cannot be known, faith germinates when we give way to what can be known: a resurrection, teachings and actions of God's love, a human—Jesus—who many I love and respect call "Lord." Both the angel and the risen Christ have the women carry a message to the disciples: to see him, you must go. Act on faith, and you will see the risen Jesus. So be it for each of us.

———◆◆◆◆◆———

Doubt is not the opposite of faith, but faith's necessary companion. How have you experienced this?

Loving God, you who are faithful to your human children, thank you for the gift of faith, for the signs of your presence and love, especially yourself in Jesus.

EASTER SUNDAY: GOD WITH US

Read Matthew 28:11-20. *"And remember, I am with you always, to the end of the age"* (v. 20).

MY PARENTS TAUGHT EACH ONE OF US CHILDREN the same night-time prayer routine. "Now I lay me down to sleep . . ." which was followed with, "God bless Mom and Dad, Grammy . . ." and so on through the immediate family, and a few others for special attention. Our prayers ended with one verse of a hymn:

> *Abide with me, fast falls the eventide.*
> *The darkness deepens; Lord, with me abide.*
> *When other helpers fail and comforts flee,*
> *Help of the helpless, oh, abide with me* (LBW , #272).

It may be the earliest thought about God embedded in my being. Even before I quite knew what the words meant, the seed of God's abiding love was planted.

The last words of Jesus were among the first given to me: "I am with you always." I see the traces of Jesus' promise to be with us always in many places along my spiritual path. We sang "Abide with me" at my brother's funeral, and again for each of my parents' funerals. The message of Psalm 8 sounds a clear note when its beginning and ending registers: "How excellent is your name, your very being, your presence, in all the earth." The Beatitudes are a declaration that God is with us, never departs; even when life seems to fall apart, God is there. It was years before I understood the source of my resonance with a native American language for God: "the spirit-that-moves-in-all-things." It is what Jesus leaves us with: I am with you, always.

It is also how this story began. Immanuel. God with us. Born into human history. Not distant, but intimate—knowing every fiber of our being. Not past only, but our present strength and our future hope. Not an unmoved mover, but a passionate lover. Not indifferent, but tender. Not an abstract force, but a willful presence of love.

It is possible for us to understand the power of the last words Jesus spoke to his disciples. We know what it means to us when a best friend moves, when a soulmate dies, or when our beloved is gone for an extended time. Our thoughts and hearts reach out to them. Their physical absence intensifies their importance in our lives.

Jesus' followers gathered with their beloved one last time. The promise, "I am with you always," was treasured by them—first as a promise and hope, then, with the spirit's arrival, as certainty and joy. There would never be anything like having his physical presence. But Jesus' love and wisdom and strength and mystical presence would never leave them.

We are also disciples who listen to the words of our beloved Jesus and feel his presence. Jesus comes to us through the words of the Gospels and in the lives of those who touch us with his love. Our minds awaken to his coming because our hearts have always known his presence. Jesus told us truly: I am with you always. Just as God has, is, and always will be with you, with love. Always.

Think of someone you miss. Picture Jesus with them. Through Christ you are present also—always.

Dear God, thank you for my life. Thank you for your love. Thank you for Jesus. Always.

WORKS CITED ⌐

Anderson, Sherry Ruth and Hopkins, Patricia. *The Feminine Face of God* (New York: Bantam Books, 1991) 25.

Carson, Rachel. *Silent Spring* (Boston: Houghton Mifflin, 1994).

Endo, Shusaku. *A Life of Jesus* (New York: Ramsey Press, 1973) 24, 25.

Hill, Ruth Beebe. *Hanta Yo* (Garden City, N.Y.: Doubleday, 1979).

Lutheran Book of Worship (Minneapolis, Ausburg Fortress, 1978) Hymns 166, 119, and 272.

Montgomery, Lucy Maud. *Anne of Green Gables* (New York: Grosset and Dunlap, 1987) 223.

Shakespeare, William. *Hamlet* (London: Heron Books, 1805) 494-5.

Shakespeare, William *Macbeth* (London: Heron Books, 1805) 472.

OTHER RESOURCES FROM AUGSBURG

Journeying through Lent with Mark: Daily Meditations by Greg Weyrauch
64 pages, 0-8066-3950-4

A Christ-centered guide to the Gospel of Mark for individual, daily devotion or group study during Lent.

Journeying through Lent with Luke: Daily Meditations by Nancy Koester
128 pages, 0-8066-4065-0

A Christ-centered guide to the Gospel of Luke for individual, daily devotion or group study during Lent.

Reflecting the Glory by N. T. Wright
192 pages, 0-8066-3826-5

Fifty-three devotional readings that show how we can reflect the glory of God by living the life of Jesus in the world.